The Modern Spice Rack

Published in 2023 by Hardie Grant Books,
an imprint of Hardie Grant Publishing

Hardie Grant Books (London)
5th & 6th Floors
52–54 Southwark Street
London SE1 1UN

Hardie Grant Books (Melbourne)
Building 1, 658 Church Street
Richmond, Victoria 3121
hardiegrantbooks.com

British Library Cataloguing-in-Publication Data.
A catalogue record for this book is available from
the British Library.

The Modern Spice Rack
ISBN: 9781784885793

10 9 8 7 6 5 4 3 2 1

Publishing Director: Kajal Mistry
Acting Publishing Director: Emma Hopkin
Commissioning Editor: Eve Marleau
Senior Editor: Chelsea Edwards
Design: Stuart Hardie
Photographer: Matt Russell
Photographer's Assistant: Matthew Hague
Prop Stylist: Rachel Vere
Food Stylist: Esther Clark
Food Stylist's Assistants: Caitlin Macdonald,
Clare Cole and Jodie Nixon
Location: Nell Carde
Copyeditor: Kathy Steer
Proofreader: Tara O'Sullivan
Indexer: Vanessa Bird
Senior Production Controller: Sabeena Atchia

Colour reproduction by p2d.
Printed and bound in China by Leo Paper Products Ltd.

Modern Spice Rack

Recipes and Stories to Make the Most of Your Spices

**Esther Clark
and Rachel Walker**

Hardie Grant
BOOKS

Contents

Introduction

We wrote this book over a swelteringly hot summer. As the temperature edged toward 40°C (104°F) Rachel sought shade behind a barricade of reference books at her spice company HQ in East London, while Esther fired up the hob in her little North London kitchen and began developing and testing the recipes for this book. London was only sleeping lightly. It was too hot to do anything other than doze – and, as dusk finally fell, the smells of the city drifted through flung-open windows: the smoke from Turkish mangals, spiced meat cooking on oil-drum barbecues and a fug from the street-food vans of melting-pot London.

It's a city with a long and complex relationship with spices. During the Elizabethan Era (1558–1603) spices flooded into London's docklands. The appetite for nutmeg, black peppercorns and cinnamon was insatiable. Few recipes were published which weren't heavily spiced and Elizabethan cooks would have been well-acquainted with nutmeg graters, pestles and mortars. It was an age of exploration, and also exploitation. Fortunes were made from forging new trade routes and growing regions were plundered, devastated by rampant greed.

Such is the fickle nature of taste that the frenzy for spices started to wane. It wasn't long after the end of Elizabeth I's reign that they began to fall out of fashion. Only the odd recipe for fruitcake or parkin survived. There were occasional peaks of interest in the intervening years, but by the start of the second Elizabethan Era in 1954, Britain's spice racks looked stark – just a few musty peppercorns, perhaps a tin of luminous curry powder or a nutmeg.

What change there's been over the course of a single lifetime – a revival in the old spices as well as a new cohort. Now shop shelves heave under the weight of sumac and shichimi togarashi, amchur and za'atar. Never before have we had the luxury of so many ingredients and the privilege of enjoying so many global flavours – yet without the context and broader understanding of an ingredient it's hard to get the most from it. A recipe might require a half teaspoon of sumac, but what of the rest of the jar? Without a grandparent from whom we can inherit an easy way with spices, there's wavering confidence when it comes to using them freely, outside of a prescriptive recipe.

It's this underlying lack of confidence that *The Modern Spice Rack* hopes to address. Spice company owner Rachel has provided a deep dive into the spices selected. By outlining the basic flavours and broader background of each spice, she sets out to establish a deeper understanding of their uses and potential. The recipes, developed and written by Esther, position the spices in a creative, modern context – with plenty of tips and suggested flavour pairings throughout, to encourage their everyday use.

Rachel is well placed to provide insight on the spices. One of her earliest food memories is of apricot *knödel* dumplings dusted with cinnamon and drenched with

melted butter, cooked by her Czech grandmother and mother. Decades later, working on the food desk at *The Sunday Times,* she studied the pace of change in the chocolate, coffee and tea industries – which were being transformed in terms of quality and provenance – yet noticed that the spice industry trundled on, selling jars of spices 'from multiple origins'. When travelling (once driving much of the Spice Route in a Fiat Panda from London to Ulan Bator) she'd come across spices that were far more potent than anything she could got her hands on in the UK – and it made the cassia-disguised-as-cinnamon that topped her *knödels* all the more disappointing.

She founded Rooted Spices and began importing the best spices she could get hold of, as directly as she possibly could. Since then, her days have entailed smelling and tasting upwards of 40 different cumin samples. She has hoofed shipments into the boot of her car at Felixstowe port, and can measure the precise weight of 35g (1 ¼ oz) in the palm of her hand (having hand-filled the first 20,000 tins she sold). She has cracked open nutmegs in Grenada and been led through alleyway doors in pursuit of the best za'atar. Rachel cooks on a daily basis with her young family – incorporating pinches, sprinkles and gratings of spices into every dish she makes.

Meanwhile, Esther grew up in West Sussex – not too far from the sea – and enjoyed being introduced to spices via clove-studded onions for bread sauce, cinnamon-baked apples and rice puddings topped with grated nutmeg. After training in the classics at Leiths cookery school, she became confident in the spices used in European dishes, but it wasn't until two days after graduation that she set off on a far more flavoursome path – firstly cooking in Italy (where she got a taste for sweet fennel-studded breakfast bakes, *peperoncino* and *cacio e pepe*) and then catering at weddings and travelling in northern India (returning with a healthy addiction to masala butter sweetcorn, aloo chaat and *paneer makhani*).

On becoming deputy food editor at BBC Good Food and then moving into the freelance world as a recipe writer and stylist, Esther specialised in developing recipes for the modern home cook – and found herself repeatedly drawn to her spice rack. As a cheap, healthy and immensely flavoursome ingredient, spices often hit the editorial brief. They also fitted with Esther's trademark style of simple, comforting home cooking. She works with the singular aim of ramping up deliciousness to the maximum – always spotting the beauty in the well-timed lemony pop of a coriander seed, the exciting hum of Szechuan peppercorns or the smokiness of Urfa pul biber, striving to transform a midweek staple or weekend dish into something special.

Rachel and Esther came together using the logic that they were greater than the sum of their parts. Their partnership fits with their broader philosophy on 'fusion' – which is often thought of as a 'bad word' but, at best, suggests the ability to adopt, adapt and assimilate to create something great. After all, without fusion there wouldn't be the joys of mulligatawny soup or kedgeree, jerk chicken or ramen. Ground cinnamon wasn't a mainstay of European bakers until the 12th century, chillies weren't incorporated into India's cuisine until the late-16th century. In many ways, the first Roman Brit who intrepidly seasoned his dinner with South Indian black peppercorns was a fusion pioneer.

The aim is not to undermine the integrity of any cuisine, but simply to continue in the grand tradition of spices being used generously, creatively and playfully with the single aim: 'to enhance'. In doing so, the lack of embedded culinary traditions might be seen as freeing. There is no attempt to capture or conserve recipes, but purely a desire to find inspiration from a snapshot in time and the delicious melting-pot of a modern, global city. How liberating to sprinkle a little Japanese shichimi togarashi over grilled cheese on toast, or top fried eggs with Turkish pul biber chilli – for no reason other than the pure pursuit of deliciousness.

The Basics

If you've only ever dabbled in spices tentatively, stuck to the recipe stringently and seasoned under-confidently, then today is the day that changes. Cooking with spices isn't alchemy. Cast aside any trepidation, set-up your spice rack so it's a source of inspiration and get ready to start seasoning liberally and joyfully.

How to Select Your Spices

A–Z lists of spices can be broad and exhaustive. Although tantalising, they put the reader in danger of the 'back of cupboard' syndrome, in which every spice is bought in a flurry of intent… only for the asafoetida or cloves to get slowly nudged out of sight and forgotten about until a house move years later.

We've honed in on the spices and blends most relevant to the modern cook, hoping to position them in new contexts and encourage frequent and confident use. In doing so, we've stuck (loosely!) to the school of thought that 'herbs are green and leafy, spices are dried and leafless'.

This approach immediately removed ingredients like bay leaves and lemongrass from the running, but still left a lot of scope. Tempting though it's been to delve into niche pepper varieties, as well as the delights of mace and tonka, we're keen to practise what we preach – and in doing so have compiled a list of spices and blends that we hope is manageable, accessible and suitable for everyday use.

By no means do we suggest that you buy everything at once. Take this opportunity to do a quick audit of your spice cupboard. Ditch duplicates, throw away anything too old and perhaps begin by getting re-acquainted with some of your lesser-used spices. Promote allspice and nutmeg into more regular circulation. Sure, that star anise might have been bought for mulled wine, but get into the habit of popping one or two in with a braised meat dish, a pan of roasting plums (page 202) or some buttery leeks.

A regular audit is good for keeping the contents of your spice tins fresh… and by becoming better acquainted with a more concise spice rack, it will hopefully become a source of inspiration, something you turn to ahead of shop-bought jars of sauces or the standard 'salt and pepper' seasoning. Out of anything else in the store cupboard, spices surely have the most untapped potential – start using them more, and you're only going to reap the rewards.

How to Shop

Increasingly, we know where our tea, coffee and chocolate comes from – but what about the cinnamon on our buns or the peppercorns in the grinder? Spices were once treasured commodities, imported only from the regions where they naturally flourished. Now, modern-day monopolies prioritise price point over provenance, meaning that a lot of commercial spices are of questionable quality.

Sure, the turmeric might deliver a yellow hue – but what of its subtle floral, peppery notes? Likewise, cinnamon might have a familiar flavour, but lack sweetness and those delicate, spicy top notes.

Spices thrive in very specific growing conditions. As with wine, the soil type, climate, careful harvesting and processing all impact their flavour. Those grown in rich, volcanic soil on a family-run estate with generations' worth of knowledge will benefit in a way that you really can taste.

Horticultural advances mean that spices are now cultivated far beyond the regions to which they're native. There are some upsides. The spice market was once strangulated by trading companies which controlled small and specific growing areas. Once spices were successfully propagated in new regions, the monopolies were broken, and they were democratised. Prices dropped and spices became available to more than just the super rich.

Downsides emerged, though. The sheer scale of modern production means that yield often takes priority over quality. Expansive and indiscriminate polytunnel growth props up the bottom end of the market. Corners are cut and processed spices are susceptible to fraud and adulteration with each transaction. It's a murky world, and often the spices that hide behind the vague claim of coming from 'countries of multiple origin' have changed hands multiple times and been harvested many years before they reach supermarket shelves.

There's an emerging backlash against the relentless (reckless) pace of modern monopolies. Innovation in the spice sector has seen small companies (like Rachel's Rooted Spices) start to trade in single-origin spices – using provenance to identify the best-performing regions, pushing for a more discerning approach and introducing a little more clarity. Instead of putting value on volume, the value is on steady relationships with small growers, and tracking down spices that smell as spices should.

None of it is straightforward. There's the issue of the 'organic' label – the cost of the certification is often out of reach of small farms, many of whom already follow traditional practices and so are growing to organic standards. Likewise, the 'Fairtrade' movement strives to provide opportunities for disadvantaged producers, but in doing so promotes Western employment standards that might not be applicable to remote and rural economies.

This is not to discount either certification – they have, in many (most) instances, been a force for good – but just to highlight the imperfection of the system.

In these early days, some engagement from the consumer is required, as well as the willingness to spend a little more on a product that is superior – both in terms of flavour and ethics. Spices aren't a big outlay, particularly when recipes require small quantities. It seems like a sensible place to reallocate some of your budget when they're so often the primary source of flavour in a dish.

What's more, supporting engaged companies striving to change the narrative, rather than buying from those who are focused solely on profit and mass-production, is a big step in the right direction (see page 224 for a list of recommended retailers).

How to Store

Spices are a store-cupboard powerhouse, and should be shown a little love. If lockdown cooking taught us one thing, then it was perhaps the value of having some decent spices to hand when faced with vast quantities of rice, pasta and tinned chickpeas (garbanzos). This is not to suggest that drastic action is needed – but perhaps add a 'spice rack audit' to that list of kitchen jobs on a fixed rota: clean the refrigerator, sort the pantry, refill the dishwasher salt. Each time the clocks change, try and carve out 10 minutes to check in on your spices to make sure that everything is present, fresh and raring to go.

1. Ditch the decades-old spices

If your spice drawer feels dated, then you're in good company. When Rooted Spices first launched, they ran a competition challenging customers to send in photographs of their oldest spices. The 'winner' (a hollow victory, if ever there was one) had dug out some cloves from 1981 (though all that was known of some undated allspice from 'West Germany' was that it was pre-fall of the Berlin Wall!).

The good news is that old, even ancient, spices are unlikely to have any ill effect. They aren't dangerous, but they are fairly pointless. Spices that far exceed their best-before date will have lost their potency and will fail to deliver the flavour hit they should. At best, they're a futile addition, and at worst, they might take on a bitterness or astringency.

There's no need to be too ruthless. Spices that are a few months past their best-before date might be revived by toasting them in a dry frying pan (skillet) until aromatic; they can then be ground and used as soon as possible. The decades-old jars of spices should be thrown out, though. Considering how little spices cost in relation to most ingredients, it's worth using some that have been harvested within the last couple of years in order to deliver the flavour hit intended.

2. Store spices away from heat and light

It's tempting to show off bright yellow turmeric and red-hot paprika in glass jars, but resist! Spices might be some of the most beautiful ingredients in the kitchen, but when exposed to direct sunlight, heat and humidity, oxidation is accelerated, bleaching the spices and causing them to lose their potency.

The effect is similar to the difference between a green cardamom pod and a white cardamom pod – the flavours will be muted and the colours less vibrant. Best practice is to store spices in opaque containers, tins or jars that are kept away from sunlight (such as in a cupboard or drawer). Spice carousels are fun to spin, but when the contents of glass jars begin to fade, the spices definitely aren't so fun to cook with.

3. Avoid 'back-of-the-cupboard syndrome'

Coming up with a good way to display your spices will go some way towards preventing them from getting lost for years at the back of a cupboard. Pull-out drawers are a good idea (though only if your spices are labelled on the lids); wall-mounted spice racks are also a great option, as are tiered shelf organisers.

Not only will well-organised spice storage help you to keep track of what you've got, but it will also inspire regular use. If everything is rammed into the corner of a pantry, then it's less likely to be used than a set of neatly organised spices that is in your eye-line when cooking. Not next to, but near the oven is best – that way, you'll be more tempted to reach for a pinch of something, and your dishes will be all the more delicious for it.

How to Cook

1. Grinding

Pre-ground spices are readily available, but grinding your own will always result in more vibrant and fresher flavours. It also allows the cook to control the size of the grind, to suit what they're cooking – for example, a fine powder is quickly absorbed into a sauce, while a coarser grind creates texture and pops of flavour.

One option is to go down the route of a hand-held electric spice grinder or coffee grinder. The advantages are speed and ease – at the press of a button, you can whizz up a blend in seconds. The disadvantages are that many are set to create only fine powders and will limit you to dry ingredients.

Traditionalists will favour a pestle and mortar. These come in a variety of shapes, sizes and materials: limestone, cast iron, granite, olive wood, betel nut wood, bronze, porcelain. All are effective, though many favour hard materials over more porous wood or porcelain. Designs range from flat grinding stones (like the decorated *shilnora* stone tablets used in

Bengali kitchens) to deep, narrow-necked mortars, which are perfect for bouncy seeds. Larger, wide-mouthed designs, such as the Mexican *molcajete* or a Japanese *suribachi* (mortar) and *surikogi* (pestle) have the additional advantage of accommodating spice pastes and salsas, as they can fit bigger ingredients like fresh ginger, coriander (cilantro) stalks, shallots, tomatoes or avocados.

Note: If toasting the spices, it should be done before grinding them – while they are still whole (see below). Fine powders or the craggy edges of roughly ground spices will burn.

2. Toasting

Some recipes give instructions for spices to be toasted. Other times, it's a matter of personal judgement. Toasting revitalises old spices and heightens (though shouldn't dramatically alter) the flavours already there.

'Toasting' should only be done with whole spices, as powders are too susceptible to burning. Ideally, each variety would be toasted separately, or in a specific and set order, as smaller seeds will toast faster than larger spices.

Simply tip the whole spices into a dry frying pan (skillet), without any oil, and heat gently, agitating from time to time to ensure that the spices are evenly exposed. Depending on the spice, the colour might deepen, though it shouldn't darken too much. Your best guide is your nose – once the air becomes fragrant, tip the seeds out of the pan to stop them from cooking.

3. Blooming

'Blooming' is, quite simply, sizzling spices in fat. It opens them up and gently teases out the flavour. Goulash, for example, might have a dollop of sour cream and a sprinkle of paprika on top, but that's purely aesthetic – the flavour comes from the paprika that is bloomed in butter, oil or lard at the start.

It's a spice-cooking technique that is used globally, with a number of different spices and fats. In Italy, fennel seeds might be 'bloomed' in olive oil when making a ragu, and in Malaysia, a spice paste might be 'bloomed' in refined cooking oil. In southern India, the fat might be coconut oil, while in northern India, it might be ghee, but the premise remains the same.

Different spices might require slightly different treatment (which should be specified in recipes). For example, paprika scalds easily, so the pan should be taken off the heat when it's added to the fat, while ground coriander can withstand longer cooking times. To stop the spices from burning, it's key to have a liquid to hand to quickly halt the cooking – for example, you can pour coconut milk, chopped tomatoes, wine, stock or even a squeeze of lemon over the bloomed spices.

4. Tempering

Much like 'blooming', the art of 'tempering' enlivens the spices, making them as vibrant as possible. The difference is that it's always done at the end of a recipe, and with urgency and ferocity. In essence, to 'temper' spices is to agitate them in hot fat, and then stir them through the finished dish. In India, this method is known as *tadka* (as in tadka dhal), *tarka* or *chhonk*, and aromatics are often included alongside the spices, like curry leaves and whole dried chillies.

In South East Asia, a *rayu* (a chilli oil that might contain crunchy garlic, ginger, peanuts and spring onions/scallions) is a similar concept. In many ways, the act of making a herb brush to baste a steak in flavoured butter is a tempering of sorts.

Tempering is a fun way to experiment with layering flavour – and a big step up from the standard salt and pepper seasoning. There's little tradition of tempering in Europe's culinary tradition, but fennel seeds, cracked black pepper, coriander seeds and pul biber chilli pepper sizzled in foaming butter and drizzled over hummus, cooked fish or a cannellini bean salad makes a compelling final flourish. (see Roast Squash, Spiced Brown Butter and Feta Yoghurt, page 172).

5. Infusing

Infusing spices in oil, vinegar, alcohol or sugar syrup is one of the simplest methods. The two scientific elements worth considering here are surface area and heat. The smaller the surface area of the spices, the faster the spice will infuse. Heating the infusion also accelerates the speed at which the spice imparts its flavour.

Whether it's a star anise added to roasted plums (see page 202), peppercorns added to vodka, coriander seeds added to a pickling liquor (see Deli Pickles, page 178) or a simple grating of nutmeg in hot milk, the results can be transformative.

6. Baking

When baking with spices, the usual techniques are either to incorporate ground spices into a batter or dough, or to use whole spices to stud the tops of breads and biscuits (cookies). From cardamom cookies (see page 192) to turmeric scones and chai-spiced pancake batter, the former technique is quite straightforward – though it should be noted that cooking spices into a batter or dough often dampens and alters their flavour profile.

When using spices as a topping it's important to make sure that small dried seeds (like caraway or coriander) don't burn by being exposed to direct heat for too long. Using an egg wash, milk or oil is a good way to make sure that they stick to the top of rolls (see page 215) or loaves.

7. Marinades and rubs

Flavour, time and technique are the three considerations when adding spices to a marinade. Firstly, will the main ingredient stand up to big spices? For example, mackerel and lamb work well with robust spices like chilli and cumin, while more delicate sea bass or scallops benefit from gentler spicing. Secondly, the time spent in a marinade will impact the spices used. For example, a piquant chilli will work well in a raw fish ceviche that might only marinate for a couple of minutes, while tandoor meats might spend 24 hours in a yoghurt-spiced marinade. Finally, consider the cooking technique. If aiming for thick, barbecue char lines, then don't be afraid to be heavy-handed with the spices, while a little pinch will go a long way in a lighter dish.

Dry rubs often darken during cooking to create a spiced crust. It might look alarming when traditional Western cooking methods precondition us not to 'burn' things in the kitchen, but the result can be delicious (see Blackened Sumac Salmon, page 122). Whether it's florets of broccoli or a piece of brisket, the action of vigorously rubbing in the spices helps the flavour to be absorbed, and the dry heat of a grill (broiler) or griddle often gets the best results.

8. Finishing

Few of us think beyond salt and pepper when it comes to seasoning. Yet shaking things up with a new finishing flavour is perhaps the simplest way of spicing a dish. Placing a pinch pot on the table – perhaps filled with za'atar, shichimi togarashi or your own 'house blend' (see page 81) – is the swiftest way to incorporate new spices into everyday eating. The key is experimentation – it's hard to go wrong. So focus on finishing a dish not with an apologetic dusting of black pepper, but with a flourish of Aleppo chilli pepper, sprinkled confidently and liberally.

Helpful recipe notes

Before you get stuck in to the upcoming recipes, here are a few handy bits of information to bear in mind.

Effort levels
Easy – Speedier recipes, fewer ingredients and an overall shorter 'hands-on' time.
A little effort – Slightly harder, but still achievable for any home cook with a few more ingredients and a little more time.
A weekend challenge – For a more confident cook or when you have a little more time to spare.

Sugar
Use caster (superfine) sugar unless otherwise specified.

Grinding
You can grind in a pestle and mortar or spice grinder unless otherwise specified – the coarseness of grinding will also be specified in the recipe.

Eggs
Size of eggs is usually specified, but if not, then always use large, and always try to buy free-range or organic.

Salt
Flaky sea salt is preferable (such as Maldon), except in cases where a 'fine salt' or rock salt is specified.

Ingredients
Use fresh ingredients unless frozen, dried or tinned are specified.

Sweating onions
A lot of the recipes start with frying an onion. Always fry it for the length of time specified, as this will cook it out properly. Don't be tempted to cut the time down, even if 10–12 minutes seems a lot.

Chopping
Finely chopped = 5 mm (¼ in)
Roughly chopped = 1–2 cm (½–¾ in) cubes
Sliced = 5 mm (¼ in) slices
Thinly sliced = 2 mm (1/16 in) slices
(on a mandolin, if you can)

Frying of spices/tempering
Don't cut down the time on frying spices, as in some cases the spices need to be cooked out properly.

Seasoning
Recipes will specify when seasoning with black pepper is required. Otherwise, 'seasoning' only refers to the use of salt, as the addition of pepper may compete with other spices. If you're browning meat, never season it with pepper before cooking, as it burns easily at a high heat and becomes bitter.

Using spices in salads
If you're adding whole spices to salads, such as fennel seeds or coriander seeds, they will need to be gently ground in a pestle and mortar first. It's a great way to release their flavour while still retaining some bite and texture.

Oven temperature
These recipes were tested in multiple ovens, but as ovens vary so much, it's important to have an oven thermometer to keep track of the temperature. A good Celsius and Fahrenheit thermometer is all you need.

Deep-frying
Invest in a cooking thermometer for deep-frying (temperature probes are particularly good), and always keep a tight-fitting pan lid nearby for safety.

Scaling up or down
Most recipes can be doubled or halved easily.

Shelf life
Most storage information is indicated in the recipes. Any baked goods must be stored in an airtight container in a cool, dark place. Anything refrigerated or frozen needs to be kept, covered in the refrigerator.

Covering
If the recipe indicates covering something, it's best to use cling film (plastic wrap) or ideally sustainable wax wraps.

Measurements
1 tablespoon = 15 ml
1 teaspoon = 5 ml

Stand mixer
This can be replaced with an electric hand-held whisk if the whisk attachment is being used. If the dough hook is being used, the kneading can be done by hand – just add an extra 5 minutes to the kneading time.

Removing spice stains!
Yes, that's right – we've all been there and ruined a crisp white shirt while cooking.

- Use a piece of sticky tape to dab at the stain to remove any dusty residue.
- Use a damp cloth to dab off the excess.
- Mix together 1 tablespoon baking powder and 1 tablespoon warm water in a small bowl, then use a small brush or old toothbrush to make circular motions on the stain for around 1 minute. Leave to stand for 10–15 minutes, then wash on a low heat.

Spices

Allspice

As its catch-all name suggests, allspice is a berry that shares flavour notes with 'all' kinds of different spices – predominantly clove, with a hint of nutmeg, black pepper and cinnamon. It has a cosy, cold-weather association – the sort of spice that often lies redundant until talk turns to pumpkin pies and 'mulling' – but get to grips with allspice, and you'll reap the benefits year-round.

The spice is ground from the dried, unripe berries of Jamaica's pimento tree. It's the only spice that is native to the Western Hemisphere, and as a result it didn't reach European kitchens until the end of the 15th century, via Spain's early ventures to 'The Americas'.

Its story is set against the backdrop of European spice consumption reaching a fever pitch, whereby Italian explorer Christopher Columbus had set out to find a direct sea route to India – in hope of accessing its treasure trove of peppercorns. Only he headed due west and arrived at the Caribbean instead.

In a fit of denial, Columbus insisted he'd reached a remote part of the Indian coastline (something he remained adamant about until his death). He referred to the group of islands as the West Indies and, on being introduced to Jamaican allspice in 1494, he declared that the dark, dried berries were, in fact, Indian peppercorns. The Spanish court (who had sponsored the voyage) humoured him by calling the dried berries 'pimento'. The botanical name *Pimenta dioica* stuck and to this day, allspice is often referred to as 'Jamaican pepper'.

Allspice berries were quicky adopted by renaissance cooks. After all, cinnamon and nutmeg laced many a European dish and the familiar flavour profile soon saw allspice added to game pies, pickling liquors, meat brines and glazes. As trade routes took it further afield, it wound up in Finnish and Swedish meatballs (*lihapullat* and *köttbullar*) and Westphalian German beef stew (*pfefferpotthast*) – and over time its sweet notes were harnessed in desserts like spiced marble cake and Yorkshire curd tart.

It's in these meaty dishes or wintery desserts where allspice remains in Europe's collective memory. Yet, (as is often the way), inspiration can be found by heading back to source where allspice is enjoyed in a very different culinary context. In Jamaica's cuisine it's used in a colourful array of warm-weather dishes: escovitch fish (often snapper, served in a spiced, pickled sauce), goat curry, sweet potato pudding

"[Jerk is] one of the enduring legacies of the fusion of African and Taíno cultures in Jamaica.

Carolyn Cooper
(Jamaican author and essayist)

Did you know?
The Arawak* word for allspice-cured meat was *boucan*. As this was part of the staple diet for Caribbean seafarers, it evolved into the word 'buccaneer'.

*Indigenous people of South America and the Caribbean.

Buying guide
Quality allspice has a warmth and roundness about it – poor-quality samples are more abrasive, and may even have a soapy note. The dried berries are so hard, an industrial grinder is best, so buying pre-ground is the way to guarantee a fine and consistent grind. Jamaica, Mexico and Honduras have long been big growers. Early attempts to cultivate the trees in Indonesia failed, although horticultural advances now mean that India, China and Peru are global players.

Culinary confusion: Allspice vs Mixed spice
The lingering demand for 'mixed spice' creates even more confusion surrounding the ambiguously named allspice. To clarify, 'mixed spice' is a curious blend of predominantly sweet spices. A quick trawl of supermarket shelves shows that it contains anything from cinnamon to cloves, caraway to coriander, allspice and the occasional dill seed – all in wildly varying ratios. Mixed spice rarely appears in recipes now, perhaps because of the unpredictability of its taste (pity the home cook who adds a teaspoon of a dill seed-heavy mixed spice blend to a rice pudding). Allspice, on the other hand, is ground from allspice berries, and is its own entity.

and black cake, as well as cocktails spiced with 'Pimento Dram' (a rum liqueur flavoured with allspice and sugar cane).

Then, most importantly, there's jerk. It's the name of both Jamaica's national dish and an allspice-based blend which, most traditionally, is used to dry-rub wild pig before cooking it in a pit. It's an early fusion dish which is thought to have evolved throughout the mid-17th century.

Its roots began with the descendants of enslaved West Africans who had been transported to Jamaica by Spanish colonialists. When the English took the island from the Spanish in 1655, many people fled into Jamaica's mountainous interior, where they became known as 'Maroons' (derived from the Spanish cimarrones, meaning 'mountaineers'). Already, Jamaica's indigenous Taíno community were in hiding (by this point, 90 per cent of them had been killed for their land or wiped out by European illnesses) – and so both persecuted groups began cooking allspice-rubbed meat in smokeless pits in the ground, to conceal their location.

'Jerk' remains embedded in the island's cuisine. It's something of a national pastime in Jamaica, and for homesick Jamaicans overseas longing for a taste of home. The recipe has travelled and continued to evolve over centuries, but ground allspice and scotch bonnet chillies remain the non-negotiable cornerstones of a jerk blend (thyme and ginger are also often added). Chicken and fish are often jerked too, and if the occasion doesn't call for jerking a whole pig, then smaller joints or pieces are the way to go, using a rub or marinade inspired by the core flavours (see Spiced Honey Scotch Bonnet Ham with Pineapple Rice, page 134).

It's these warm-weather dishes which open up new possibilities for a tin of allspice. Thinking of it in the same breath as rum, pineapples and bananas will breathe life into this often-neglected spice (see Spiced Rum Sticky Toffee Pudding, page 186). After all, allspice is not just for Christmas – even in the European kitchen it's the differential in a good tomato ketchup, gooseberry chutney or carrot cake. It's not as sweet as cinnamon, is more versatile than cloves and deserving of much more prominence in ingredients list.

Amchur

Amchur (or amchoor) is a spice on the move – from the marginal to the mainstream. It's long been available in Asian supermarkets, but a growing interest in regional Indian dishes has propelled this dried green mango powder into cookbook ingredient lists. It's got a lot going for it: a tangy-sour brightness with resinous notes. Though rarely a lead flavour, it brings a hard-to-pin-down liveliness to dishes.

Traditionally, amchur is used as a souring agent in the Hindi Belt – particularly round Uttar Pradesh and Bihar, the heartlands of India's mango orchards. During peak mango season, the fruit is eaten fresh: cut into cubes or fingers and sucked from the stone (pit), leaving forearms sticky with the juice. It is also (as Madhur Jaffrey describes in her memoir), served seasoned with salt, pepper, cumin and red chilli.

As with most delicacies, there is a catch. The season is short. There's a fleeting window of perfect honey-ripeness, and mangoes don't travel well. So, rather than subjecting them to a bruising journey, canny mango growers came up with a way to preserve the fruit. Mangoes are picked while still green and unripe, and strips of their flesh are dried in the sun. These are then ground into amchur, which works year-round as a souring agent – used much like yoghurt and tomatoes in North Indian cuisine, and tamarind and raw mango in the south. Amchur is quite different to freeze-dried ripe mango powder. Don't expect anything amber-coloured or mango-sweet. Picking the fruit before it ripens means that it's tart, and sun-drying the flesh drains it of any colour leaving it an uninspiring shade of beige. The powder might not look like much, but looks can be deceiving.

It's a key component in a *chaat masala* spice blend, which is used in a lot of street food: *bhel puri*, samosas, *aloo chaat* (see page 130). It's often used in a Punjabi *chole* or chana masala chickpea curry (see page 100). It usually appears as a background flavour, but if you find yourself tearing apart a paratha to mop up the last vestige of a dish, then it's often the amchur that has made it taste so authentic, so alive.

As amchur travels outside the central Hindi Belt, its uses become more diverse – from Southern Indian *rasam* (spiced soup) to Indonesian *serundeng* (crisp coconut topping). It's early days in terms of amchur's broader adoption, and there's fun to be had – try making Sweet and Salty Cashews (page 176), or concocting a spice blend (amchur, scant cayenne pepper and ground black pepper) to pep up an apple juice, banana and spinach smoothie, harnessing that bright sourness in a creative new way.

Buying guide

Quality amchur can be judged by its bright flavour. It should be kept away from moisture at all costs, as it will form clumps that need to be bashed apart with a wooden spoon or pushed through a sieve (fine mesh strainer).

Did you know?

Amchur is so high in vitamin C it has been used in the treatment of scurvy. The combination of jaggery (unrefined cane sugar) and amchur proved to be effective in combating symptoms.

Caraway Seeds

Did you know?
Caraway seeds are often used in a Middle Eastern harissa paste. The seeds are also ground for a popular dessert eaten over Ramadan called *meghli* – a spiced pudding made from rice flour and topped with nuts.

There are few spices that have fallen foul of fashion like caraway seeds. Up to the mid-17th century, they were cherished in the kitchens of medieval Europe. No wonder – caraway seeds have the earthiness of cumin, but they're more amenable and sweeter, with liquorice notes and a lemon-peppery brightness.

Tudors feasted on caraway seed cake and caraway-flavoured 'jumbles' (sweet biscuits/cookies). The seeds were sugar-coated and used as 'kissing confits' to sweeten the breath. It's extremely rare to find caraway used in sweet bakes now – not unless they're being made to summon a taste of the past. More fool us! The dried seeds are a magical ingredient, particularly when used alongside ground almonds (as in a traditional seed cake) and paired with lemon icing.

One reason that caraway is – rightly – muscling its way back into kitchens is, perhaps, the repositioning of Eastern European and Balkan cookery. There's passion for pumpernickel, a keenness for krauts. Cooks are bigging up brassicas, and there are few better ways to celebrate a cabbage than the introduction of caraway seeds. Whether it's cabbage coleslaw, slow-braised cabbage, stir-fried cabbage or sauerkraut, it's a match made in heaven.

Historically, it was the easy accessibility of caraway seeds that entrenched them in Northern, Central and Eastern European and Balkan cuisine. It's a home-grown crop, which thrives in cooler climes where days are often short and dark. Scandinavia remains a big producer. It's useful to think of these growing regions when getting creative. Caraway seeds instantly elevate some of Europe's less fashionable veggies: carrots, collard greens, cabbage, kale (see Caraway Greens and Sausages, page 110). The seeds feature in Jewish dishes (salt beef, rye bread, borscht) and specialist cheeses, such as Danish Havarti, in which caraway's anise bite cuts through the richness.

The other medium in which caraway might appear on the table is in bottled form. Caraway-flavoured spirits were, until recently, considered pretty obscure and steeped in faded grandeur: Kümmel swigged by European hussars, aquavit ('snaps') sipped by Norse nobles. Changing tastes have seen bottles appear more regularly on digestif menus. It signals a full circle for the spice, which was first recorded as being something to soothe flatulence and aid digestion (in the Ebers Papyrus, 1550 BCE). It seems fitting that over three millennia later, caraway-flavoured spirits are making a comeback – sipped after an overindulgent meal to help stave off symptoms of excess.

Cardamom

Cardamom summons the opulent and exotic flavours of the spice route: saffron jewelled rice and pistachio *kulfi*, Indian chai, blush rose syrups, *qahwa* coffee and dates. Its resinous, honeyed scent is found in the markets of Samarkand and Turkish souks, and features in many dishes from places that dot the old trading routes.

It might then come as a surprise to learn that Guatemala is the world's leading exporter. The crop wasn't introduced there until 1914 – but the plants flourish in the humid cloud forests of both Guatemala's Highlands. Orchid-like stalks stretch up to 4 metres (13 feet) in the air, and branches laden with pods (also referred to as 'capsules') erupt from the plant's base.

Cardamom is known as 'green gold'. It's the third most expensive spice in the world after saffron and vanilla, and is labour-intensive to harvest. Skilled pickers have to differentiate raw and ripe pods, which often sprout on the same branch and are similar shades of green. Once dried, the pods are rigorously graded based on size, weight and colour. 'Extra bold' or 'extra jumbo' seeds (8–9 mm/⅜ in) burst with fragrant seeds and command top prices.

The story of cardamom in Guatemala is not dissimilar to that of nutmeg in Grenada. Both are 'Old World' spices (native to India and Indonesia, respectively), which were introduced to the 'New World' in the nineteenth and twentieth centuries. They flourished and have become integral to local economies. The difference is that while nutmeg was embraced by Grenadian cooks (nutmeg chicken, nutmeg ice cream), in Guatemala, cardamom remains a pure commodity.

It might not have been adopted by local cooks, but cardamom is actively sought after in cuisines worldwide. In Norway and Sweden, the per capita consumption is sky high. It goes into gravlax cures and pickles, cardamom buns (*kardemummabullar*), cardamom cake (*kardemummakaka*) and rolled cardamom wafers (*krumkake*). The recipe for White Chocolate, Espresso and Cardamom Cookies (page 192) captures that distinctly Nordic way of using cardamom's big flavours in sweet bakes.

The story is that the Vikings first discovered Indian-grown cardamom in Constantinople when trading in the Byzantine Empire (modern-day Turkey). It's certainly the most likely route for cardamom to have made it to Scandinavia, and it can be traced through all manner of recipes: first Indian chai, biryani rice and curry mixes, and then, as caravans moved through the Middle East, there's jewelled rice, Persian chicken, halva Adeni tea (*shahi haleeb*) and the Turkish tradition of adding cardamom pods to the coffee pot.

The magpie nature of British cuisine has seen also cardamom creep into more fusion-style dishes over the years: cardamom rice pudding, cardamom sponge cakes, cardamom-spiced fruit crumbles. It's a beautiful flavour when added to poached rhubarb or apricots (see page 89). The recipes for Apple Cardamom and Custard Doughnuts (page 189) and Mango, Coconut and Cardamom Bircher Muesli (page 86) show the sheer versatility of this beautiful spice and its ability to casually enliven a dish.

Cardamom pods
Use whole pods to infuse liquids (from savoury sauces to poaching liquors, hot teas and milk). Bash them with the flat side of a knife or a rolling pin to crack them open and release more flavour.

Cardamom seeds
Use the tip of a knife to flick the grey-black seeds out of the pods. Grind them with a pestle and mortar to create a powder, which can then be added directly to batters and dough. Depending on the dish, it's useful to add a pinch of salt or sugar when grinding.

Black Cardamom and White Cardamom
Black cardamom is the larger relative of green cardamom, and is used predominantly in savoury Indian dishes. It's dried over an open fire, which darkens the husk and gives it a bold, smoky flavour. White cardamom is a bleached version of green cardamom. It has a pale husk and more muted flavours. One theory is that the chemical bleaching process replicates the way the pods were sun-bleached on long boat journeys, and curbs the flavour for markets which were used to receiving a gentler version of the spice.

Avocado and House Blend (page 81) on toast

Orange and red onion salad with fennel seeds

Chillies

There are few ingredients more versatile than the chilli. It's the spice in Szechuan hotpots, fiery Indonesian sambals and South Indian sambars. It's the pinch of paprika on devilled eggs, the dash of Tabasco in a Bloody Mary and the gentle heat of a chilli jam. It's responsible for the utter devotion inspired by a peri peri chicken, and for the violent, mind-blowing heat of a curry house *phaal*.

In truth, dishes laced with chillies are eclectic, infinite, global. Yet the one thing that unites most is they are relatively recent developments. The earliest account of chillies being used in a culinary sense is from 5000 BCE in Mexico, but it was only some 500 years ago that Columbus sailed back from 'The Americas' and presented chillies to the Spanish court.

Up until then, all African, Asian and European cuisine relied on black pepper, ginger and mustard seeds for a fiery sensation. How quickly things changed. With it being 'The Age of Exploration' and burgeoning trade routes, chillies infiltrated cuisines worldwide within a few short decades, and changed the way that people ate forever.

Chilli crops were planted throughout West Africa; they survived Indian monsoons and thrived in kitchen gardens throughout Southern Europe. Cooks who'd been subjected to the frenzied inflation of tropical spices suddenly had an attractive alternative. Chillies were easy to grow, they were cheap to buy and they imparted an almighty kick.

Mexico remains a place of pilgrimage for true chilli connoisseurs. Selecting and cooking with one of the country's 200 varieties (ancho, de arbol, guajillo and piasilla, to mention a few) is something of an art form. They are used for flavour as much as singular hotness. Indeed, it's common for a traditional mole sauce (a *mole negro*, for example) to contain upwards of six different chilli varieties, none of which are interchangeable. They're bred for complexity: fruitiness, sweetness, or notes of chocolate, molasses, raisin or tobacco. Some are smoked, some are sun-dried; some are mild and others eye-wateringly hot.

The traditional way of cooking with Mexican chillies is to buy them whole and dried. Home cooks will then laboriously toast, rehydrate, de-vein and seed them. Pre-ground powder or flakes present a speedier option. A pinch of ancho chilli powder will bring mild, fruity heat and cacao notes to a chilli con carne or *xocolatl* hot chocolate. The Slow-cooked Ancho Beef Shin on page 137 is inspired by the slow-cooking of a traditional barbacoa, while the recipe for

Did you know?
Chilli heat is measured in Scoville heat units (SHU). This is a useful resource if you want to gauge how hot a recipe will be, or if you're looking to make substitutions. Woe betide anyone who substitutes a teaspoon of Kashmiri chilli powder (2,000 SHU) for a teaspoon of cayenne pepper (50,000 SHU)!

When it all changed
'The pepper which [the locals] use as spice is more abundant and more valuable than either black or melegueta pepper [Grains of Paradise].' – New Year's Day, 1493. Columbus's diary entry, written from his ship, *Niña*, moored off Haiti, in which he discovers chilli peppers.

Ancho Prawn, Fregola and Charred Corn Salad (page 148) showcases this mild but immensely flavoursome chilli in a fresh context.

In terms of ramped-up chilli heat, India's cuisine is world-renowned. It's the biggest producer, consumer and exporter of chillies worldwide, with 75 per cent grown in the south-eastern state of Andhra Pradesh. India's cuisine has less specificity than Mexico's – chilli's purpose is more for heat than flavour.

There are hundreds of different varieties throughout the country, from the ferocious Naga Viper, which measures 1.3 million SHU (see opposite), and is used to infuse cooking oil in the north-eastern state of Nagaland, to the cherry-shaped Salem Gundu grown in Tamil Nadu. Thin-skinned chillies might be ground into a powder (so that they absorb quickly into a sauce), while thick-skinned varieties might be kept whole and used for tempering a dish at the end of cooking, along with mustard seeds and fresh curry leaves.

In India, there's no such tradition for recipes to specify a particular chilli, although a growing interest in regional cuisine is changing this. Instead of lumping in generic hot chilli powder, recipes might, for example, specify Kashmiri chilli (or *deggimirch*), a bright and mild heat that doesn't overpower. It's a popular variety throughout India and brings beautiful warmth, as demonstrated by the recipes for Sweet and Salty Cashews (page 176) and Paneer Makhani Pie (page 163).

From Indonesia and Thailand to Ghana, Ethiopia and China's Sichuan and Hunan Provinces, it's typical for chilli-loving cuisines to lie close to the equator. Many are united by starch-heavy diets (rice and wheat), which are enlivened by a chilli kick. It's interesting that, despite Europe being the 15th-century launch pad for chilli's takeover, only a light touch of chillies made its way into European cuisine. With the exception of Spanish and Hungarian paprika, as well as a small amount of chillies used in Portugal and Southern Italy (Calabria), throughout most European cuisines, Old World spices (black pepper, cinnamon, fennel, coriander) predominate.

In Britain, it wasn't until the waves of Indian immigration in the 1950s and Caribbean immigration in the 1960s that 'hot' spicy food started being cooked on these shores. Now, it seems like we're catching up on lost time. From sausage rolls to scotch eggs, chillification is rife. Whether it's a sweet chilli or hot pepper sauce, a squirt of sriracha, a spoonful of kimchi or some lime pickle on the side, the lust for a little chilli kick knows no bounds.

Note
Paprika (page 56) and pul biber (page 60) are two chilli varieties often specified in recipes – so we have given each one their own entry in *The Modern Spice Rack*.

Cinnamon

If there's one spice you shouldn't scrimp on, it's cinnamon. There's enormous variation within the category – at one end of the spectrum is the delicate fragrance of 'true' Sri Lankan cinnamon, and at the other end is the cheapest ground cassia, which may even be laced with powdered beechnut husk.

Confusion between the two fragrant barks goes back almost 2,000 years. The Greek physician, Galen (129–216 CE), pointed out that 'the finest cassia differs so little from the lowest quality cinnamon that the first may be substituted for the second, provided a double weight be used'.

It's not to say that there's anything wrong with cassia bark. It's robust and sweet, forms a key component of Chinese five spice and is often used in slow-braised savoury dishes. It's just that it isn't cinnamon, shouldn't be labelled as such, and often is. It's why the word 'true' increasingly precedes the word 'cinnamon' (or 'verum' after) to show that it's *Cinnamomum zeylanicium* – the real deal. Delicate, fragrant and woody-sweet.

There's little dispute that the best-quality cinnamon is grown in Sri Lanka, although there's some confusion as to whether this is where the spice originates. There's evidence of cinnamon being used in Ancient Egyptian embalming rituals – and one school of thought is that as early as 2000 BCE it was traded from South East Asia to Madagascar along the East African coast and into the Nile Valley. 'Sweet-smelling cinnamon' is referenced in the Bible and was, by then, a common ingredient throughout the Middle East.

It wasn't until the 12th century that cinnamon arrived in British kitchens, thanks, most likely, to the Crusades. Around then, dishes developed a Middle Eastern flavour, often featuring meat cooked in spices and fruit. *The Forme of Cury* (1390) features a recipe for rabbit or kid goat served in a red wine vinegar sauce with onions, currants, ginger and cinnamon.

Over time, cinnamon moved from main course to pudding, and by the Georgian period it was predominantly used in a sweet context: honey and cinnamon tart, spiced pears, set custards and bread-and-butter pudding. Across the Atlantic, cinnamon remains largely seen as a sweet ingredient (with the exception of the Thanksgiving staple, sweet potato casserole). Cinnamon toast and apple pie topped with cinnamon sugar have a near-ritualistic appeal in parts of America.

Did you know?
Cinnamon once grew wild. The Portuguese established mass plantations on the southern tip of Sri Lanka – the most accessible point by sea. It's where most crops remain, but there's an emerging interest in 'wild' cinnamon grown Sri Lanka's Central Highlands, which has less sweet, spicier notes thanks to the maturity of the trees.

Meanwhile, British cooks have been influenced by Ottolenghi's culinary crusade, and a revival in Middle Eastern cooking has seen a full-circle move. Tagines, and even Moroccan *pastilla* (a savoury pie topped with icing/confectioners' sugar and cinnamon) or Iranian *fesenjan* (a chicken stew flavoured with walnuts, pomegranate and sweet spices) have helped reposition cinnamon in a savoury context. The recipe for Slow-cooked Lamb with Prunes and Harissa (page 140) is meltingly beautiful, and a perfect example.

Trade routes transported this spice around the world, and it's fascinating to see how different cuisines adopted it. There's cinnamon in Mexican mole sauce, Greek-Cypriot *avgolemono* (chicken and lemon) soup, Swedish cinnamon buns and Austrian *marillenknödel* (fruit dumplings, which are dusted with cinnamon and then drenched in hot butter). It's one of the trickiest spices to put in a specific box when it comes to cuisine or sweet and savoury use, which makes it all the more freeing to cook with, considering the infinite possibilities offered by a single pinch.

Buying guide

Cinnamon sticks: (also known as quills) are harvested from the inner bark of the cinnamon tree, which is peeled and dried in rolls. It's distinguished by the multiple tissue-thin layers (almost like furls of millefeuille) that curl round to form a single quill. Multiples are sold in 'bales' and the thinner the quills' diameter, the higher the price. The Sri Lankan system has four grades, from 'Alba' (less than 6 mm/¼ in diameter) to 'Hamburg' (less than 32 mm/1¼ in diameter).

Cassia bark: is harvested in the same way to cinnamon sticks, but once dried it forms a thicker bark that often curls into a single furl. It's more red-brown in colour and has a more robust flavour.

Cinnamon quillings: are shards of cinnamon bark (under 10 cm/4 in long) which are a by-product of peeling, cutting and baling cinnamon. They're dried and still have a culinary use, although cost around 25 per cent of the price of cinnamon quills. Quillings are also sorted into grades, with the most intact quillings commanding the highest price.

Cinnamon featherings: are pieces of inner bark made from peeled twigs or stalks rather than the main trunk, and may contain a percentage of cinnamon chips (see below).

Cinnamon chips: are an unpeelable combination of inner and outer bark that can't be further refined. Rather than wasting them they are dried like cinnamon, sold for less than 10 per cent of the price, and are often infused into cinnamon bark oil.

Coriander Seeds

As spices go, coriander seeds are usually part of the orchestra rather than the lead soloist. The mellow, citrus note runs through Indian garam masala, North African berbere, Mexican mole and Vietnamese phở. They're used in pickles (see page 178) and brines, and frequently appear as a botanical in gin, providing an understated spiciness. Present, but barely discernible.

The seeds vary in size and colour, from pale green to straw and nutty brown, depending on the soil type – they thrive in hot, dry climates where the sunlight and lack of water intensifies the flavour. As with most seeds, dry-toasting and grinding them on demand gets the most out of them, but particularly with coriander, the grind size can really alter the flavour. Things start to get exciting when the seeds are roughly cracked or sprinkled whole as a finishing flavour, creating lemony bursts (see Pepperonata, Coriander Seed, Charred Tomato and Burrata Salad, page 139) or even crackled in a little oil or butter and drizzled over a dish, tadka-style (see Roast Squash, Spiced Brown Butter and Feta Yoghurt, page 172).

Coriander is native to Southern Europe and the Mediterranean. Remains of the spice were discovered in Tutankhamun's tomb and 'manna sent from heaven' is described as being 'white like coriander seeds' in the Old Testament. Its modern name derives from Ancient Greece (*koris*, meaning 'bug'*) and there are references to coriander seeds throughout the Roman cookbook *Apicius* – where it's found in Alexandrine-style pumpkin and sauces to accompany boiled fish. The vast array of historical references hint at its abundance in the ancient kitchen.

The presence of coriander seeds has endured throughout the cuisines of the Eastern Mediterranean, North Africa and the Middle East. It's in falafel, harissa and dukka (the Egyptian nutty spice mix). It's particularly popular in Cypriot cuisine, where recipes like *elies tsakistes* (cracked green olives with whole coriander seeds), *afelia* (red wine and coriander pork) and *lountza* (cured pork tenderloin rolled in coriander seeds) give it a prominent position.

On arriving in India, coriander seeds were embraced. Despite it already being home to so many hardworking spices, they quickly became an essential part of masalas, commonly used in conjunction with cumin. Ground coriander is often the first spice added to the pan after onions – needing the longest to cook out – and it's believed to curb the spiciness of a dish. From *khichdi* (a South Asian rice and

Did you know?
Coriander was used to flavour the earliest form of beer, invented in the third millennium BCE by the Sumarians in Southern Mesopotamia (modern-day Iraq). The technique has been revived and coriander seeds are commonly used in Belgian witbier, such as Hoegaarden or Blue Moon Belgian White.

*Coriander contains aldehydes, organic compounds also found in soaps and, strangely enough, in stink bugs (shieldbugs). The ability to detect the smell is genetic, so only those born with the required olfactory receptors are able to make the link between coriander smelling bug-like (or tasting soap-like).

lentil dish, see page 113) to *kadhi* (a Rajasthani yoghurt-based curry) and *koththamalli* (a curative Sri Lankan tea), it forms the backbone to a wide range of recipes throughout the Indian subcontinent.

It's a spice defined by its versatility. Coriander seeds might flavour a main course (see page 112 for Crispy Pork Belly) or a dessert – perhaps a honey cake with orange and coriander seeds. Whole seeds might pack a punch as a finishing flavour, or subtly support, as with the classic French dish vegetables à la Grecque, where a well-timed pinch of coriander is barely discernible, but cleverly enhances what's already there.

Plums poached with star anise

Cumin

Of all the spices in the spice rack, cumin shouts the loudest. Its big, earthy aromas are unmistakable. It's one of the most-used spices in the UK, with a strong presence in modern, mid-week repertoires: a pinch of ground cumin can be found in curries, chillies, fajitas and burgers.

Perhaps its ubiquity is in danger of robbing cumin of any sense of the exotic. Or perhaps it's the coarsely-flavoured varieties that make their way on to supermarket shelves that do it a disservice. For anyone who thinks that all cumin tastes the same, it may come as a surprise to learn that there's enormous breadth within the category. Some seeds are bitter, astringent, overpowering, but those with a warmer, toastier flavour will reignite a sense of excitement when reaching for a tin. Its deliciousness should make you feel like you could use it as a stand-alone seasoning, not just in a walloping meat rub.

Cumin is native to North Africa and the Middle East, and its presence is still strongly felt there. In Morocco, it's not uncommon for a pinch pot of freshly ground cumin to be placed on the table alongside the salt. Dishes there are generously spiced with cumin, which stands up to big flavours: slow-cooked lamb, aubergine (eggplant) *zaalouk*, spiced fish stews. Cumin runs through Middle Eastern pastes (harissa, zhoug, chermoula) as well as the region's spice blends (*advieh*, baharat, berbere, ras el hanout).

In India, cumin is big business. The country is the biggest global producer, but also the biggest consumer – with as much as 80 per cent of its enormous harvest catering for the domestic market. Crops thrive in the western states of Gujarat and Rajasthan. Tiny pink-white flowers bloom under a scorchingly hot sun, and quickly give way to small, beautifully flavoured seeds. Those grown in the desert tend to have a particular delicacy, a brightness. They hold their own in the robust, tandoor-meat dishes of northern India, but also work when a light touch is used, happily topping a salty lassi (see page 92) or *jaljeera* (a popular drink flavoured with roasted cumin).

Although cumin is a primary flavour in India (one of the 'big four' alongside ground chilli, turmeric and coriander), heavy use of the spice extends to a culinary belt spanning Central Asia, from Kazakhstan, Kyrgyzstan, Tajikstan, Turkmenistan and Uzbekistan, to Nepal, Mongolia and North-west China. It works well with rich, fatty, full flavours, such as Xinjiang's cumin lamb, Uzbekistan's *plov* and Nepal's *momo* dumplings (see also Spicy Chilli Oil and Cumin Lamb Noodles, page 114). The lighter, more delicate dishes of South East Asia (laksa, hoppers, sambals, pad Thai) are far more sparing with their use of cumin, if it appears at all.

The 'Cumin Divide' (as we shall now call it) continues across other continents and cuisines. It's a flavour that is intrinsic to West Africa (*maafe* peanut stew, goat *shoko*), but while Cajun and Creole cuisines share an enthusiastic use of chillies, cumin is absent from spiced dishes like jambalaya and gumbo. In Mexico, a light touch of cumin is used in enchiladas, chilli con carne, carnitas (pulled pork) – but, with the exception of Tex-Mex dishes, the use of cumin stops at the northern border.

In Europe, cumin was used widely in Roman kitchens (when it was imported from Ethiopia, Syria and Libya), but with the collapse of the Roman Empire and its trade routes, the spice broadly fell out of favour, and locally available caraway was used instead. The Moorish influence in southern Spain (from the 8th to the 15th centuries) saw cumin imported for dishes like *pinchitos* (kebabs) and Seville's trademark orange and cumin marinade (often used with chicken and pork). Latterly, European cheese-makers embraced the spice, with Dutch varieties like Gouda and Leyden setting cumin against beautifully pale, milky, fatty flavours (see Gouda and Cumin Butter Biscuits, page 214).

It's now become a cornerstone of modern cooking and is the second most-used spice worldwide (after peppercorns). Whether cooking Middle Eastern, North African, Latin American or Indian dishes, a tin of cumin is rarely far from hand. It does the heavy lifting in spice blends, props up pastes and can be used as a finishing flavour, whether it's seeds crackled in a tadka or ground and stirred into a yoghurt dip. A well-timed pinch of cumin goes a phenomenally long way.

Fennel Seeds

Fennel is the only spice that might be nibbled straight from the tin. There's something soothing about the green, sweet-anise seeds, and so evocative – for some, it might prompt a memory of fennel tea or fennel-studded breads, while for others it might conjure recollections of leaving Indian restaurants with sticky pink and yellow candied fennel seeds (*mukhwas*), used to sweeten the breath.

Recipes that call for 'fennel' often refer to the bulb, which looks like a swollen celery heart. It's a divisive ingredient that people tend to find either divine or disgusting. If you're in the latter camp, then don't discount fennel seeds. They're gentler and sweeter. Give them a chance by grinding a few seeds with sugar and then sprinkling them over strawberries to explore their sweet, herbaceous notes (see Macerated Strawberries with Fennel Seeds, page 98 and Strawberry Fennel Seed Ice Cream, page 197).

Fennel grows indiscriminately throughout Europe. Fronds sprout like weeds and billow out into umbrella-shaped seedheads, which self-sow on roadsides, scree slopes and arid patches of land. The Eastern Mediterranean is a big producer, as the hot sun swells the plump seeds. Once harvested in late summer, they are gently dried to retain a bright green colour and capture a sweet, piney flavour.

It's an ingredient with a curious history, moving in a counter direction to most of the spice trade. Fennel is native to Europe and wasn't incorporated into the Indian pantry until long after its early European references. Some of the earliest recorded recipes containing fennel are found in *De re coquinaria* (a 4th- or 5th-century Roman culinary compendium). It includes a recipe for fennel-roasted pork loin, a dish from which a modern-day porchetta is descended, as well as fennel-spiked sauces for boar, venison and veal.

The Italian love of fennel has endured. Even when Venice was the pulsating heart of the spice trade, with caravans of far more exotic ingredients passing through, Italian cooks only really embraced black peppercorns, nutmeg and latterly chillies. Instead, native fennel remained a firm favourite. There's *finocchinona,* (a Tuscan salami dating back to the late Middle Ages), *brodetto* fish stew, meat ragus and *polpetta* studded with fennel (see page 145 for 'Nduja and Fennel Seed Meatballs). There are fennel *taralli* biscuits (cookies) in southern Italy, *finocchietto* liqueur sipped as a digestif along the Sorrentine Peninsula, and the Tuscan tradition of boiling chestnuts in fennel-flavoured water.

When the seeds travelled eastwards, they became a popular ingredient. Fennel features in the spice blend *panch phoran* (used throughout north-eastern India, Bangladesh and Nepal), as well as Chinese five spice. Long before scientists discovered that fennel seeds' primary compound, anethole, is 13 times sweeter than sugar, cooks recognised that the seeds' natural sweetness was useful in balancing out blends and offsetting bitter and savoury notes.

In modern British cooking, it's rare that fennel seeds are integral to a dish, but a well-timed pinch can be transformative. In winter, the dried seeds might be added to sautéed mushrooms, used in a rub for slow-cooked pork belly, or in an orange and chicory salad. In the summer, a few fennel seeds will lift a mussel broth, a tomato sauce and any seafood cooked with chilli or lemon zest. Its amicability with citrus extends into desserts, and a Fennel Seed and Lemon Buttermilk Pound Cake (see page 210) is a teatime triumph – positioning this European spice in the most British of settings.

Garam Masala

Garam masala is an enigmatic spice blend. There's no singular use and no standard recipe. Its origin story has no linear narrative. In many ways, it's infuriating, when a prescribed 'pinch of garam masala' leads dishes down such wildly different paths. Its fluidity is, however, quite fitting, and something to be embraced. After all, India's cuisine is a tapestry of different tastes. Why expect a standardised blend from a country where the cuisine can change over the course of a half-hour train journey?

In truth, the only thing that unifies garam masala is the fact that no two are the same, although a loose set of rules seem to apply. It's rare for chillies to be used in a garam masala. Sure, its name roughly translates as 'hot spice blend', but the heat traditionally comes from peppercorns and other spices that are classified as 'warming' in an Ayurvedic* sense: ginger, cloves, cardamom.

It's also rare for a garam masala to contain turmeric. This might come as a surprise to Brits who grew up with yellow-hued Coronation chicken made using a curry powder. The two blends are quite different, though, and not to be used as substitutes. Curry powder is an Anglo-British creation (a turmeric base, often with chillies and asafoetida) while garam masala is a gentler, fragrant blend (often with a peppery heat and woody-sweetness).

It's common for Indian households to batch-make their own garam masala from handed-down recipes, shrouded in ritual. First, they toast each spice in a set sequence – an intuitive process, where the spices that need cooking the longest are flung into a dry pan first. As soon as the kitchen starts to fill with an aromatic fug, the spices are quickly cooled, ground, sieved (strained) and stored in an airtight container. Elaborate recipes might contain exotic ingredients, from saffron to stone flower (an edible lichen), but garam masala is predominantly mixed from everyday spices and used as an everyday blend. Delhi-based food writer Marryam H. Reshii's family recipe uses equal amounts of green cardamom, cloves and cinnamon; she references a chef from Uttar Pradesh whose garam masala consists of just cardamom and mace.

Fragrant blends like this are often used at the end of a dish, with the tiniest pinch added as a final aromatic flourish. However, in the UK, garam masala is often enlisted to do a lot of the heavy lifting at the start of recipes, and it is usually cooked off with the onion-garlic-ginger base. Perhaps it's down to the spices used in commercial

* Ayurvedic medicine is an ancient and holistic Indian medical system, still practised to varying extents by 80 per cent of the population in India and Nepal. It's based round the concept that illness is caused by an imbalance. Integral to the underlying belief that everything is connected is the idea that foods can be grouped in a certain manner (for example, 'heating' or 'cooling') and used to readjust a person's balance.

Did you know?
It's interesting that lots of the components used in garam masala are not native to India (often only peppercorns and cardamom). For this reason, it's thought that garam masala was first used by royal palaces, which could afford to import exotic ingredients, before blends were adopted by home cooks and adapted to suit the flavours of their regional cuisine.

blends – three out of Britain's 'Big Four' supermarkets use a coriander-cumin base for their own-brand garam masala, neither of which are at their best when sprinkled raw.

It's advisable to either use a consistent recipe or always buy from the same brand so you know what you're working with. That way, you'll become familiar with the flavour and confident in adjusting amounts appropriately, allowing you to experiment beyond biryanis, korma, saag paneer and lentil dishes. Try adding a pinch over vegetables (like carrots or parsnips) before roasting them, introducing a little to the base of soups or even for spiced beans on toast.

There's a long history of Anglo-Indian fusion: kedgeree, mulligatawny, Coronation chicken (for a vegetarian twist, see Roasted Cauliflower Wedge Coronation Salad on page 166). The marriage of British and Indian flavours is ever-evolving and increasingly present in modern recipes – and there's no easier way to summon that than with a well-timed pinch of garam masala. It will jazz up a cottage pie or scotch egg; it won't overpower, as a harsh curry powder might, but will instead enliven and enhance.

Noodles with broth and shichimi togarashi

Olives with extra virgin olive oil, fennel seeds and coriander seeds

Ginger

There are lots of different forms of ginger: fresh ginger (the knobbly root), pickled ginger (to accompany sushi), crystallised stem ginger (soft and sugar-coated, like fruit pastilles) and stem ginger in syrup (sticky, floating orbs). In terms of the spice rack, we're talking dried ginger – an unassuming, beige powder.

The edible root is native to South East Asia, where it's predominantly used in fresh form in dishes like Singapore chilli crab, Malaysian laksa, Indonesian *semur* (stew) and *kinilaw* (Filipino-style ceviche). Much like turmeric and mango, the flavour profile of ginger changes during the drying process. In the case of ginger, the clean heat is tempered into something warmer, spicier and more nuanced.

Different varieties of dried ginger sit somewhere on a broad spectrum – from having an almost perfumed, peppery heat to a fierce spiciness. Sri Lanka and South India have become big producers. In Tamil Nadu (India's most south-eastern state) dried ginger has worked its way into a chaat masala (spice blend), masala chai (spiced tea), *rasams* (spiced soups) and *sambars* (lentil-vegetable stews).

During the drying process, ginger loses 80–85 per cent of its weight, making it a spice that travels well. Throughout Medieval Europe, it was the second most popular spice (after black pepper), and lots of historic recipes have lasted the test of time. There's Austrian *lebkuchen* (similar to German *pfeffernüsse* – small, iced/frosted ginger-spiced biscuits/cookies), Dutch *speculaas* (spiced shortcrust biscuits/cookies) and French *pain d'epices* (a ginger-spiced loaf). In the north of England, there's parkin (a ginger cake made with oats and molasses), as well as Grasmere gingerbread (made with dried ginger and nutmeg).

Perhaps most famous, though, is plain gingerbread – be it a gingerbread house or gingerbread figurines, which date back to Queen Elizabeth I's court (1558–1603). It's said that the royal cook shaped gingerbread into silhouettes and decorated them to resemble important guests. By the late 16th century, such was its broad appeal, gingerbread was even referenced in Shakespeare's *Love's Labour's Lost*: 'An I had but one penny in the world, thou shouldst have it to buy ginger-bread.'

It was round this time – 'Peak Gingerbread' – that the root began being cultivated in the West Indies, making it one of the first spices to be

Ginger Jars

Now they're most often used as lamp bases, but highly decorative ginger jars were once used for storing and transporting spices. They date back to the Qin Dynasty (221–207 BCE), but first arrived in Europe in the early 17th century, filled with Chinese ginger preserved in syrup. The high-shouldered, dome-lidded jars are highly collectable thanks to the elaborate motifs painted on the sides – particularly those with a reign mark on the base, showing who was Emperor at the time of production.

successfully transplanted from the 'Old World' to the 'New World'. Jamaica became a big grower and began exporting ginger to Europe as early as 1547. It remains a flavour integral to the island's cuisine, be it a slice of Jamaica ginger cake (see page 194 for Spiced Molasses Banana Cake and Cream Cheese Frosting) or a swig of Old Jamaica ginger beer.

Dried ginger remains in everyday use along the ancient trade routes. It's often the 'fifth' spice in a Chinese five spice (occasionally substituted for Szechuan peppercorns) and regularly features in a Middle Eastern baharat blend. Yet in European kitchens, it often gets shoved to the back of the spice cupboard until December, except the odd ginger biscuit (cookie) or gingersnap. More fool us. A well-timed pinch can add a kick to fish and meat cures (see Spice Rack Cured Salmon, page 93), carrot or squash soups, a batch of marmalade, plum crumble or roast figs. In the recipe for No-bake Salted Ginger Caramel Chocolate Tart (page 198), fiery ground ginger plays an integral role in tempering the chocolate-caramel sweetness.

It's a spice that brings balance, both in terms of balancing flavour and also more broadly restoring equilibrium. The King's Ginger liqueur was a 'fortifying beverage' prescribed by King Edward VII's physician, and many a seasick passenger's stomach has been settled by a nibble on a ginger biscuit (cookie). Stirring a pinch of dried ginger into honey and pouring over hot water makes for an uplifting start to the day, and – particularly with a nip of whisky added – is a soothing way to round off an evening too.

Mustard Seeds

There's Dijon mustard sold in crested crocks, German mustard in glass beer steins and silver mustard pots adorning tables dressed for a Sunday roast. There's American mustard squirted over hot dogs and English mustard spread on slices of pork pie – not to mention the black mustard seeds that crackle in tadka pans throughout India. Whatever the cuisine, whatever their guise, these potent little seeds pack a punch.

Did you know?
Recipes for the condiment 'mustard' date back to the Roman era, when ground seeds were mixed with grape 'must' (fermented juice) – hence the name 'mustard' (must + *arden* meaning 'to burn').

Mustard seeds are an ancient and much-loved spice – harnessed for their heat long before chillies were globally available. They have a nostril-tingling potency and a peppery-heat which opens the sinuses and prickles the eyes, much like wasabi and horseradish (also in the Brassicaceae family). The seeds are inert and odourless until cracked or ground, and mixed with a liquid (vinegar, wine or beer).

Yellow mustard seeds predominate in European cuisine. Their mild heat flavours condiments (piccalilli, *mostarda di frutta*) and they are largely used as a pickling spice. There's such an abundance of quality mustards available, there's little point making it from scratch – adding a dollop straight from the jar to a stew or vinaigrette does the trick.

It's India's creative use of brown and black mustard seeds which make this such an interesting spice. They might appear in breakfast dosas, pickles (see page 178) and even drinks (*neer mor* spiced buttermilk). They are a frequent finishing flavour, thanks to the tradition of crackling mustard seeds and fresh curry leaves in an intoxicating hot oil tadka (see Crispy Curry Leaf Roast Potatoes, page 175).

Interestingly, one region where mustard seeds are not used so much in a tadka is Bengal – which is otherwise responsible for a frenzied use of mustard in almost all other mediums. In this most north-eastern state, almost everything is cooked in mustard seed oil, accompanied with *kasundi* (mustard ketchup), or flavoured with freshly-ground mustard seeds which are added straight to the pot.

Bengal's use of mustard demonstrates how these flavorsome seeds might be incorporated into everyday cooking. Look to its famous mustard fish curry (shorshebata) for inspiration when cooking seafood. Crackling mustard seeds in hot oil to dress cooked potatoes, roast cauliflower florets or green beans will instantly lift a side dish – and mastering the art of a simple mustard seed and curry leaf tadka is a way of transforming even the most humble of lentil dishes into something a bit special.

Did you know?
Canada's mustard exports make-up around 80 per cent of the global supply, with the majority coming from Saskatchewan Province's prairie-grown mustard seeds, which are cultivated over an area the equivalent of 115,000 football pitches.

Nigella Seeds

Did you know?
Nigella seeds are a unique source of thymoquinone – 'an emerging natural drug with a wide range of medical applications' (Mohannad Khader and Peter M. Eckl, *Iranian Journal of Basic Medical Sciences*, 2014) – whose potential benefits were re-examined in regard to the prevention and cure of COVID-19.

Of all the spices in the spice rack, nigella seeds are the most rooted in folkloric medicine. Their old Latin name, *Panacea*, roughly translates as 'cure all', and the seeds crop up in the medical scripts of most major civilisations, appearing in Greco-Roman, Jewish and Ayuverdic texts, and mentioned in Islamic medicine (*Tibb-e-Nabawi*), with Prophet Muhammad describing them as a 'remedy for every disease except death'.

In an age of modern pharmaceuticals, we now turn to medicine cabinets for solutions ahead of spice racks. However, an increasingly holistic approach is catapulting spices with health-giving properties into more regular use. If the explosion of turmeric turned all sorts of unexpected foods bright yellow (see page 76), then it's not too much of a leap to expect beautiful black, tear-drop-shaped nigella seeds to adorn more dishes in years to come.

It's certainly no penance. Nigella seeds have a wonderful, nuanced flavour: oregano-herbaceous notes with a gentle, charred-onion bitterness. They come from Nigella sativa, which is a flower in the Ranunculaceae family related to 'love-in-a-mist' (popular in country gardens and wedding bouquets). Unhelpfully, they have been given a host of misleading names, including black onion seeds, black cumin, fennel flower – and when sprinkled, are easily mistaken for black sesame or poppy seeds.

Nigella seeds are more than just a seasoning within Middle Eastern cuisine, from where they are thought to originate: they are infused in the pickling liquor for preserved lemons and used in Syrian string cheese (known as *tresse* cheese or *jibneh mashallah*). In India, nigella seeds (*kalonji*) feature heavily – studding naan breads, used in chutneys and potato dishes, as well as being one of the five spices in the popular Bengali blend, *panch phoran* (along with fennel, fenugreek, cumin and mustard seeds).

Nigella seeds are excellent when sprinkled liberally over savoury bakes, from bagels to *böreks*, sables to scones. The flavours work well with a mature cheese, particularly a barrel-aged feta or mature Cheddar (see Warm Cheddar and Nigella Seed Buns, page 215). Fresh or dried herbs bring out the oregano notes – a pinch pot of nigella seeds with sage and mint is a beautifully fragrant summer blend – and nigella seeds are a wonderful way to season roasted vegetables. Even if they don't cure you of *all* ailments, the flavour alone will certainly put a spring in your step.

Did you know?
As late as the 1970s, nigella seeds were absent from Western spice compendiums, making them a relative newcomer to spice racks.

Nutmeg

There are few better illustrations of 'the rise and fall' of spices than nutmeg. Once, cookbooks were crammed with recipes that called for lavish amounts – a heady grating of nutmeg indicated wealth and refinement. Yet now, it's scarcely nudged into the spotlight outside a few winter warmers – béchamel sauce and bread sauce, milk-based puddings and Brandy Alexanders – and the use of mace has all but disappeared from the modern kitchen.

To stand in a nutmeg forest is to be reminded what a loss nutmeg is from daily cooking. The air is filled with a spicy-sweet scent. Apricot-sized fruit hang from the trees and break open like conkers. First, there's the cream-coloured padding, known as 'pericarp', a fruity flesh that is often turned into jams or syrup by cooks who have access to fresh nutmeg. Then, nestled within is a single mahogany-brown kernel, wrapped in a leathery red mace web. Once harvested and dried, nutmeg can transform a dish. The swiftest grating, a mere whisper, can turn anything from a hot buttered crumpet to a bowl of porridge (oatmeal) into something sensational.

Nutmeg's story centres round an obscure volcanic archipelago in the easternmost reaches of Indonesia: the Banda Islands. Ostensibly once the world's only source of nutmeg, the islands became the setting of some of the worst atrocities of the spice trade. For centuries, nutmeg had been harvested and traded peacefully (most likely shipped in outrigger boats to join the main overland spice routes), but once European powers got involved, frenzied greed and corruption meant that within a few generations, the tropical paradise had been plundered.

The Portuguese were the first to lay claim to the Banda Islands (after discovering a sea route in 1512, round the Cape of Good Hope). Almost a century later, the English and Dutch arrived, all guns blazing, with the Dutch eventually taking control. So began a period defined by brutality and paranoia. Anyone suspected of smuggling samples off the island was threatened with the death penalty. Nutmeg kernels were dipped in lime to stop them sprouting and, in Amsterdam, nutmeg warehouses were burned to keep prices artificially high. By 1621, only 600 of the native Bandanese (from a pre-conflict population of 15,000) were thought to have escaped execution or expulsion.

The monopoly was, eventually, broken by a one-armed, amateur botanist, a roving Frenchman called Pierre Poivre. He got hold of nutmeg kernels from some disaffected Dutchmen and transplanted

Did you know?
Nutmeg wasn't propagated in Grenada until the mid-19th century, but by the turn of the 21st century, 30 per cent of Grenadians' income was linked to nutmeg production. The small island (whose population is roughly 1/82 that of London) is responsible for approximately 20 per cent of the global nutmeg supply.

Did you know?
In the 16th and 17th centuries, nutmeg morphed into something of an aspirational fashion statement: poseurs carried silver, engraved nutmeg graters to align themselves with the exotic commodity and ensure they were prepared for any nutmeg eventuality.

Did you know?
In the seminal 18th-century cookbook, *The Art of Cookery Made Plain and Easy* by Hannah Glasse (1747), there are 318 references to nutmeg – for example, in a recipe for 'plain cheesecake' which calls for a whole nutmeg to be grated into the eight-egg recipe.

them to a botanical garden in Mauritius. It was the first of several successful propagation attempts. The price soon began to tumble. Nutmeg had lost its exclusivity and status, and fast fell out of fashion. By the Georgian period, heavily spiced nutmeg dishes had become passé.*

There were pockets of exception, which have endured. In Italy, the love for nutmeg runs deep – from *malfatti* dumplings to cannelloni and tortellini fillings (in which nutmeg is often paired with spinach, pumpkin and ricotta – see page 150 for Spinach and Nutmeg Gnocchi). New growing regions welcomed nutmeg into their cuisine, too. It became an important crop in Grenada (it was introduced in 1843, just before myristica blight devastated the Banda Island plantations) – there, it's celebrated in chicken stew and nutmeg-flavoured ice cream.

Unlike Europe, with its fickle palate, the ancient growing regions and trade routes have stayed more loyal to nutmeg. It's integral to Indonesia's *semur babi* (nutmeg pork stew) and *semur ayam* (nutmeg chicken stew). In India's cuisine, nutmeg is frequently used in conjunction with mace, cinnamon and cloves to flavour biryani, korma and rogan josh. In the Middle East, it's often seen in baharat spice blends, Lebanon's seven spice blend and ras el hanout.

There's some irony in the fact that although nutmeg stars in few mainstream European recipes, it flavours Coca-Cola and Pepsi – continuing that medieval nutmeg addiction in a very different guise. It's an ingredient that should be celebrated, not surreptitiously sipped. A quality nutmeg has a brightness, almost an effervescence, and such beautiful aromas. The best thing to do is to place one on the kitchen table, along with a grater, to encourage frequent use: spinach omelettes, French toast, Welsh rarebit, cheese soufflés, oat muffins, squash soup, oxtail stew, peach cobbler – get a taste for it, and soon, perhaps, you'll find yourself seasoning dishes like a Jacobean.

Did you know?
Nutmeg is thought to be an aphrodisiac. It's also known to be a powerful narcotic. Beatniks chased highs at 'nutmeg parties', where they'd eat several tablespoons of the ground spice – something Malcolm X remembered when serving time in Charlestown Prison in 1946: 'My cellmate was among at least a hundred nutmeg men who, for money or cigarettes, bought from kitchen worker inmates penny matchboxes full of stolen nutmeg. I grabbed a box as though it were a pound of heavy drugs. Stirred into a glass of cold water, a penny matchbox full of nutmeg had the kick of three or four reefers.'

*See *Satire III: The Ridiculous Meal* (1665) by French writer, Boileau, in which the unrefined host is mocked for serving heavily spiced, *ancienne cuisine*: 'Do you like nutmeg?' he asks the guests, who have barely touched their meal. 'It has been put into everything.'

Golden blend porridge

Crumpets with butter and grated nutmeg

Paprika

Unlike most spices, the story of paprika is not one of trade routes and taxation. After Columbus first introduced capsicum peppers to Spain's Royal Court in the late 15th century, they were passed over to monasteries in the Extremadura region – a south-western area of Spain bordering Portugal. The monks successfully grew them in their own kitchen gardens, and soon local farmers started planting crops.

It was a culinary turning point. Up until then, expensive and imported black peppercorns had been the most popular way to spice up a dish. Suddenly, Spanish families could plant chillies in their back gardens and get a serious punch of flavour from home-grown produce. No wonder paprika so quickly worked its way into the heart of the country's cuisine and has remained there ever since.

Chilli varieties like Bola and Ocales thrived in Spanish soil, but there was one big stumbling block when it came to processing them. Unlike in the tropics – where spices are largely sun-dried – Extremadura's late harvest season coincided with heavy rainfall (the average October rainfall matches that of London). So, the tradition emerged of slowly drying the chillies over a fortnight in smokehouses instead, infusing them with distinct oak-woody notes.

Now the artisanal practice is tightly controlled and protected. The region of La Vera (a county within Extremadura) has been awarded a PDO (Protected Designation of Origin), meaning that all the paprika produced there is made in a traditional way, even down to the stone mills that grind the dried chillies. La Vera paprika is exported worldwide. Traditionally, the sweet-smoked varieties would be used for lighter dishes – chicken, fish, rabbit – while the hot-smoked varieties are used in charcuterie (chorizo, sobrasada) and heartier winter stews.

It'd be wrong to think of paprika purely in a Spanish context. A Hungarian proverb sums up the passion that paprika rouses in Eastern Europe: 'One man may yearn for fame, another for wealth, but everyone yearns for paprika goulash.' It wasn't until the late 19th century that the spice became popular in Hungary, but, since then, there's been some making up for lost time. Not only are paprika shakers often placed on dining tables, but paprika chilli peppers are also minced (ground) and sold in jars (*erős pista*) or puréed and sold in squeezable tubes (*piros arany*) so a quick squirt

Paprika glossary

Spanish paprika
Dulce: sweet and mild
Agridulce: bittersweet, medium heat
Picante: hot
Ahumado: smoked
Pimentón: Spanish word for 'paprika'

Hungarian paprika
Édes: sweet and mild
Csipős: hot
Különleges: 'special quality' (often vibrantly coloured, finely ground, mild in flavour)

Did you know?
Hungarian-style *chicken paprikash* was popularised in the late 19th century when legendary French chef Auguste Escoffier put *poulet au paprika* on the menu at the Grand Hotel in Monte Carlo.

Tip
Unhelpfully, recipes don't always specify what type of paprika to use – frustrating when varieties range from mild to very hot. The best strategy is to look at the amount used. If it's anything more than a teaspoon, it's unlikely to be a picante, as the fiery varieties have a real kick, so go with a dulce or agridulce instead, for a gentler fruity heat. In terms of labelling, if a tin simply says 'paprika' without specifying the variety, it's most likely to be a sweet Hungarian-style paprika – mild and unsmoked.

can be administered in a second to spice up a stew (*pörkölt*), or fisherman's soup (*halaszlé*), or even be mixed with soft cheese and spread on toast (*korözött*).

The most common and traditional way of cooking with paprika is to add it to hot fat near the start of a recipe. Whether stirring it into a Spanish sofrito (slow-cooked onions, garlic, bell peppers) or a Hungarian roux, it should be done when the pan is off the heat. Paprika burns easily and will darken and turn bitter if cooked too harshly or at too high a temperature. Sprinkling it on a cold dish will impart colour and give a hint of aroma, but by no means will it allow the paprika to bloom and reach its full potential.

From spicy chorizo to romesco and *bravas* sauces, there's a wealth of Spanish recipes in which paprika plays the starring role, and likewise with Hungarian *paprikash* and goulash. Its uses have diversified as paprika travelled – a pinch for spicing burgers, biltong, blackened salmon (see page 122) – and they continue to evolve. The boom in meat-free dishes often harnesses smoked paprika's ability to impart an almost bacon-like substance and robustness, which goes a long way in a cauliflower spice rub, vegetable fritters (see page 104) or cowboy beans. It's not always about a whack of flavour; sometimes it's the subtly smoky undertones or mild fruity heat that makes this the secret weapon of the spice rack, and a go-to if you need to rescue a pallid chicken stew or bland bean burger.

Peppercorns

Glass shakers of pre-ground pepper seem only loosely related to the oil-rich, dark peppercorns that grow on vines throughout Southern India. 'The King of Spices' was once so valued it was used as currency; it paid dowries and was flaunted only in the smartest of dining rooms. Its downfall follows the broad narrative of the commercialisation of spices, but there is one difference with peppercorns – while other spices fell out of everyday use, pepper remains a go-to seasoning.

Its ubiquity does it no favours. Sure, 'season with salt and pepper' appears in many a recipe, but often it's a knee-jerk instruction. The deliberate addition of good-quality, freshly cracked peppercorns can transform a dish. Unfortunately, it's rarely included as a lead flavour and is instead often absent-mindedly sprinkled on as an afterthought, save for a handful of recipes, such as Italian Cacio e Pepe (page 111), Singaporean black pepper crab, French steak au poivre.

It wasn't always the case. In the 12th century, a pound of pepper (450g) was worth the equivalent of three weeks' land labour in Britain. The much-loved spice was grown exclusively in Southern India and was traded overland through Afghanistan and Persia, subjected to taxes and marked up with each transaction. British society was deeply divided, and spices were only available to the upper echelons, who enjoyed pepper-laden dishes that demonstrated their status and wealth.

What a loss for the majority, whose diet was very plain, very pappy: pottage and thick boiled grains (frumenty). These beige dishes must have made peppercorns an object of lust. However, the 'Pepper Divide' remained in place for the following 300 years, and little changed in terms of availability and accessibility. Venice controlled the flow of spices into Europe – two-thirds of which were peppercorns. The city grew enormously wealthy, and peppercorns remained out of reach for most.

Everything changed with the 'Age of Discovery'. European explorers saw that there was a fortune to be made by finding direct, duty-free sea routes. This goaded on the Portuguese seafarer, Vasco da Gama, who rounded Africa and arrived at India's western Malabar Coast in May 1498. On his return, Europe's centre of commerce shifted overnight from Venice to Lisbon. By evading the overland taxes, the peppercorns he brought back to Portugal were sold at one-fifth of the price of those in Italy.

Pepper glossary

Black pepper (*Piper nigrum*): grape-like bunches are picked from vines when on the cusp of turning from green to a deeper red. Sun-drying them darkens and wrinkles the outer layer and intensifies the flavour. Terroir impacts flavour: Tellicherry (India), Kampot (Cambodia) and Lampong (Indonesia) are all renowned for top-quality peppercorns.

White pepper: involves an additional process – the peppercorns are soaked, fermented and the outer layer is stripped off. The result is something milder and mustier. White pepper is often used for aesthetic reasons (for example, in béchamels, chowders, pomme purée). Sarawak (Borneo, Malaysia) is emerging as a big growing region.

Green pepper: picked before ripe and most commonly dehydrated to stop them from ripening into black peppercorns. Traditionally, green peppercorns were pickled in a brine and used in classic peppercorn sauces. Milder than black peppercorns, with bright, fruity notes.

Pink pepper: unrelated to black pepper and native to South America. Naturally oily with higher water content. Mild in flavour, with a fruity acidity and piney notes. Traditionally used in cream sauces and pickling liquors.

Did you know?
The Guild of Peppercorns was one of London's earliest livery companies, founded in 1180. It evolved into The Grocers' Company (who represented spice merchants), and is an indication of what an important commodity peppercorns were.

Once the Venetian monopoly was broken, peppercorns boomed more than ever. With the Portuguese controlling India's west coast, Arab and Asian merchants looked to Indonesia to get their stock (by this point, peppercorns were commercially grown in Sumatra). European imports rose from 2 million lbs per annum (1497) to 3 million pounds (1506), then 6 million lbs by 1570. Though more affordable, peppercorns remained a luxurious and pricey commodity. (The fact that profits were still made despite one in four ships sailing from Portugal to India being lost at sea between 1500 and 1628, hints at how lofty the margins were).

By the early 18th century, pepper had become a domestic staple – its cost in real terms was one-fifth of that in medieval times. Burgeoning availability was the death knell for most spices – once they lost a sense of exclusivity, they fell out of fashion – but the daily use of pepper endured. However, its lustre faded over the centuries that followed. The engraved silver pepper muffineers* of the Georgian period slowly evolved into glass shakers of greying ground pepper on formica café tables.

The commercialisation – even the degradation and adulteration – of peppercorns has created an emerging countermovement, a mounting interest in provenance. Buying whole peppercorns from a renowned growing region may cost a little extra, but the rewards more than justify the expense. Wine-like language homes in on different qualities to look out for: muskiness, piquancy, fruitiness, citric and camphorous notes (like menthol rubs) – each vine is impacted by its terroir. From Tellicherry to Kampot peppercorns, it's less about regional superiority and more about the fact that a single-origin peppercorn is likely to be a big step up from the tubs on supermarket shelves.

In their purest form, the best way to enjoy peppercorns is to freshly crack them (using a mill or pestle and mortar) and season meaningfully. Loosely cracked peppercorns will create bursts of heat in all manner of dishes, from a summer Niçoise salad to a wintery gratin. Whole peppercorns might be used for infusions (pickles, gin, masala chai). When it comes to seasoning meat, it's often best to do so after cooking, as cracked peppercorns will burn during the browning or frying process. Peppercorns don't require too much preparation or fuss in the kitchen – the key is good sourcing, so it's best to focus on that, because a little extra effort there will go an enormously long way.

*A pepper muffineer is the term for antique silver shakers.

Did you know?
The phrase 'kitchen pepper' is used in 18th-century cookbooks to describe cooks' everyday blend. For example, the 'kitchen pepper' recipe given by Edinburgh-based Mrs Frazer, (author of *The Practice of Cookery*, 1791) contained black peppercorns, allspice, nutmeg and cloves.

Pul Biber (Aleppo/Urfa)

In Istanbul's Grand Bazaar, alongside stalls selling copper pans and Iznik pottery, Turkish delight and fruit molasses, are mounds of 'pul biber'. It's the catch-all term for Turkey's chilli (hot pepper) flakes, which include variants such as Aleppo pepper (from the Halaby pepper) and Urfa (cultivated in the Şanlıurfa region, near the Syrian border).

The flakes are distinguished by their beautiful sheen, which, from a distance, means they resemble dried fruits (like dates or raisins) more than the paper-dry chilli (hot pepper) flakes seen on supermarket shelves. It's a result of traditional processing: the chillies are bagged and sweated so they retain their natural oils. Different varieties have distinctive colours and flavour profiles. Aleppo pul biber is a bright, orange-red with a sun-dried tomato-like fruitiness, while Urfa pul biber is a near-black, prune-like colour, with smoky, raisin-like sweetness.

Pul biber appears in few spice reference books, to date. Even as the 'Ottolenghi effect' took hold and thrust new ingredients into the limelight (*c.*2008), pul biber was still scarcely available. It wasn't until an episode of *At My Table* (2017, BBC) that it became prime time, when Nigella Lawson dropped a teaspoon of red Aleppo flakes into a pan of foaming butter to make Turkish Eggs (*çılbır*) (page 97). Thanks to cooks like Sabrina Ghayour and Selin Kiazim specifying 'pul biber' over generic 'chilli flakes' in ingredients lists, it's grown in popularity and fast earned a place in a modern spice rack.

Throughout Turkey, pul biber is used as a condiment as much as a cooking ingredient. Pinch pots sit on tables, and it's liberally sprinkled as a finishing flavour atop *lahmacun* flatbreads, fattoush salads, barbecued meats and *Ezogelin çorbası* – a traditional red lentil, bulghur and red (bell) pepper soup. Outside the Eastern Mediterranean, the bright flakes often adorn avocado toast, roasted pumpkin wedges and charred greens, such as broccoli, broad (fava) beans and griddled courgettes (zucchini), which are instantly lifted with a squeeze of lemon and a pinch of pul biber.

An exciting way to cook with pul biber chilli (hot pepper) flakes is to bloom them in hot fat, so the colour bleeds out to make a bright, spiced butter or oil. The resulting red swirl can be used in many ways, such as topping the pale yoghurt sauce that accompanies *manti* dumplings. From drizzling Aleppo pul-biber-infused oil over a bowl of hummus to seasoning a barbecued beef steak with foaming Urfa butter, it's a sensational final flourish.

When it comes to a quick sprinkle, pul biber is a great addition to halloumi and honey (see Chilli and Honey Fried Halloumi, page 182), and also happily works in lots of cheese-based contexts: with goat's cheese and walnuts, whipped ricotta, in a mascarpone-based pasta sauce (see page 120), even in a tuna melt.

Truthfully, you can't go wrong with pul biber. Its uses are endless, and whether it's a pinch over breakfast eggs or a mid-week meal of Roasting Tin Chicken with Aleppo and Lemony Butter Beans (page 128), it's advisable to keep a pinch pot of pul biber on the kitchen table, for every eventuality.

Hummus with olive oil and flash-fried fennel seeds

Cheese, honey and urfa chill

Ras el Hanout

Spice-selling is competitive business throughout Morocco, be that competition surrounding the precariously balanced conical displays or the potency of medicinal blends posturing as 'Berber Viagra' (Moroccan ginseng).

It's against this backdrop that ras el hanout (which translates to 'top of the shop') is used by merchants to showcase their best-quality spices and flex their culinary muscles. Forget 'bottom of the barrel' spices, it's only the best that go into a ras el hanout – an elaborate blend, often containing upwards of 25 perfectly balanced spices (rumours of 100-spice blends circulate, though suspiciously there are no ingredient lists to back up such claims).

There's no uniformity. Variants might be driven by regional flavour, a vendor's inherited recipe, or even their customers' budget, depending on which part of town the store is located. 'Imperial' versions might contain saffron, while another ras el hanout might emphasise floral notes, with dried rose petals, dried lavender or violet-scented orris root.

A quality ras el hanout should be light and piquant. There's bright heat from white pepper, black pepper, dried ginger and grains of paradise. There's usually sweetness from cinnamon, eucalyptus notes from cardamom or galangal, gently bitter cubeb and fragrant clove, nutmeg and allspice. More unusual ingredients might define a signature blend, like dried mountain ash (rowan berries) or monk's pepper.

Perhaps it's most helpful to look at the ingredients that shouldn't go into a ras el hanout: salt and sugar are frowned upon. Onion powder, garlic granules and more aggressive spices like cayenne and fenugreek (purists would even say even cumin) are generally omitted. It's rare for Morocco's cuisine to be singularly spicy. The key is balance – with no lone ingredient rearing its head. Ras el hanout might underpin the flavour of a lamb tagine, but it should also have the ability to flavour a spiced honey glaze for cooked fruit (oranges, pears) without imparting an overwhelming or confusing savouriness.

One origin story traces ras el hanout back to the ancient city of Sijilmasa. Centuries ago, it's said that an argument broke out between traders, which spooked the camels, who were carrying spices. The bags of spices were shaken off their saddles and split

More than two dozen spices are needed to complete the intoxicating aroma in which the nomad warrior has combined all the scents of the countries he has passed through.

Madame Guinaudeau
(author of *Traditional Moroccan Cooking*, 1958, which she wrote while living in Morocco for more than three decades from the 1930s).

Did you know?
In souks, ras el hanout is often sold whole or 'brut', as this best preserves the flavour of the spices. It's possible to ask for it to be ground, and typically the merchant will use a 'burr' (coffee bean-style) grinder. In the West, the spices are usually pre-ground, and then dried flower petals are stirred through afterwards.

open as they hit the ground, mixing together. The merchant, who had already paid, had little choice but to scrape up the spices he could salvage and rebrand it as a desirable new blend.

It's a dubious story, but there are credible parts: Morocco (and indeed Algeria and Tunisia, where ras el hanout is also popular) was integral to ancient overland spice routes. A huge range of foreign goods were loaded on to camel trains and moved from the Gulf and Red Sea across North-west Africa to Europe. The trade route has long defined the region's cuisine, along with the early Muslim conquests (7th century), which introduced a typically Persian cooking style of incorporating dried fruit, sweet spices and nuts into savoury meat dishes.

Little surprise that's where ras el hanout really sings. Whether it's chicken with dates, lamb with dried apricots or beef with figs, a bright and beautifully balanced spice blend will always enhance. Alongside regional variations, there are some enduring recipes, such as *mrouzia* (honey-spiced lamb stew with raisins and almonds) or *pastilla* (spiced squab or pigeon pie with almonds and cinnamon) as well as *tfaya* couscous, which is traditionally topped with caramelised spiced onions, honey and raisins (see page 90 for a spicy take on caramelised onions).

Unsurprisingly, the versatility of ras el hanout recipes is reflected in the versatility of its uses. This is not an 'add half a teaspoon', prescriptive kind of spice, but one where a well-timed and liberal pinch will go a long way. Try tossing some ras el hanout over root vegetables or chickpeas (garbanzos) before roasting. It will also bring beautiful flavour to a chicken and lentil soup or a griddled courgette (zucchini) salad. It might be made up of anything from eight to 80 ingredients, but one thing is certain – and that is that a great ras el hanout is much more than the sum of its parts.

Shichimi Togarashi

Shichimi togarashi has gone from obscure to obtainable within a few short years. The traditional Japanese spice blend first arrived in the UK via ramen bars and udon joints, but soon started cropping up in cookbooks. It was swiftly propelled on to supermarket shelves, and is now the secret weapon of fusion-loving chefs.

The backbone to the blend is chilli (*togarashi*) – and it should have a kick to it. *Shichi* means 'seven', and, as the name suggests, there are six more ingredients that work in perfect harmony. Dried mandarin peel creates top notes, while dried seaweed brings umami savouriness. There's a tongue-tingling sensation from ground sansho pepper, and a crunch from poppy seeds and black sesame. Traditional varieties also contain hemp seeds (perhaps incongruous in a country where possessing even a small amount of cannabis results in prison time – but toasting the seeds prevents them from sprouting or having any effect other than adding earthy flavour).

The dynamic blend appeals to modern palates, but it's thought to date back to the 17th century, shortly after the Portuguese introduced chillies to Japan. Lots of the country's most established shichimi togarashi producers started out as vendors on the *sandō* (approach) of Buddhist temples. It guaranteed heavy footfall, and also catered to those practising *kampō* – a Japanese adaptation of Chinese herbal medicine. Vendors would make up bespoke variations of the seven-spice blend to suit customers' personal tastes or to focus on specific ailments.

Now, shichimi togarashi's use is purely culinary. Shaker jars are ubiquitous throughout Japan, though the blend is generally used to season robustly flavoured dishes like noodle broths and *yakitori* grilled meat, not delicate sashimi or sushi. The recipe for Kimchi and Togarashi Fried Rice (page 117) is a good example of how it stands up against other bold flavours like pickles, sesame oil and soy.

It's a natural partner to seafood thanks to the citrus peel and sansho pepper acidity. There are few better ways to improve a grilled (broiled) salmon fillet or crayfish and avocado sandwich than with a liberal shake of shichimi togarashi. It's the crowning glory to a show-stopping Togarashi Prawn Cocktail (page 162) and brings a delicious kick to Crab and Togarashi Mac and Cheese (page 159).

Although the traditional way to serve it is a red flash of shichimi togarashi adorning the plain backdrop of rice or noodles, the versatility of this ready-made blend means it is happy in any number of scenarios, from morning to night: on top of baked eggs or around the rim of a Bloody Mary at breakfast, with fried chicken (see page 156) and a cold Japanese Pilsner-style beer, or even dressing up a bowl of late-night instant ramen.

Star Anise

The bold aromas of star anise reverberate throughout some of South East Asia's most famous dishes: Vietnam's pho noodles, *hong shao rou* (Chairman Mao's pork belly) and Chinese five spice roasted duck. Sadly, star anise never *really* caught on in Europe. Sure, it's occasionally glimpsed in a racier afternoon tea, where the damson jam or blackberry cordial might have a hint of star anise, but it's rarely used with the same passion, assuredness and ferocity as it is in Asia. In fact, so scarce is its appearance in ingredients lists, star anise was almost omitted from *The Modern Spice Rack*, but we have included it for its enormous potential.

Its complex flavour is often described as 'liquorice-like' – although that evokes unfair connotations with black liquorice, and over-simplifies its flavour profile, which is complex and herbaceous, gently bitter, with floral, eucalyptus notes. Taste-wise, there's overlap with fennel seeds – but with markedly different cooking applications. For example, dried fennel seeds bob around on the surface of liquids, while a woody star anise is more at home lurking in a dark bone broth.

The spice is native to South East Asia. There, the *Illicium verum* tree has been cultivated for more than 3,500 years – and is so treasured that there's some evidence of star anise being demanded as reparations between warring tribes. The pale yellow or vermillion, magnolia-like flowers give way to seed pods, most of which have eight prongs (or 'carpels'), each housing a small egg-shaped seed with a caramel sheen. They're harvested in both spring and autumn (fall); autumn seedpods are usually bigger and brighter-coloured, and command a higher price.

The unripe green seedpods are sun-dried into brittle, brown woody stars, which – from this point onwards – need handling very carefully. Shipments specify the 'broken rate' by percentage (the lower the percentage, the higher the price), and fragments might be grouped in 'broken only' batches that sell on the cheap. It doesn't change the taste when cooking, but using shards doesn't have the same visual appeal. After all, it's the distinctive star shape that inspires the name, both in Europe and South East Asia (Cantonese *bat gok* and Mandarin *bajiao* both roughly translate as 'eight-horned').

It wasn't until relatively late that star anise made it into the European pantry. It had long been traded along the Ancient Tea Horse Road (spiced Russian tea is flavoured with orange and star anise, and Tibetan butter tea often contains the spice too), but it first arrived in Europe in 1588, as part of Thomas Cavendish's haul. The Suffolk-born explorer (or, perhaps more accurately, 'pirate') was the first to deliberately navigate the globe (Magellan and Drake had both done so previously, but unintentionally). After more than two years at sea, he returned with a captured 600-ton Spanish galleon and looted Spanish gold, as well as silks, damasks, musk and star anise from the Philippines.

The spice was incorporated into Europe's cuisine very slowly. It occasionally features in Tudor recipes: spiced quince butter cake and a spiced hot chocolate allegedly drunk at Charles I's court. By the Georgian and Victorian periods, it was largely used in cordials and compotes – orange and star anise marmalade, plum and star anise jam. This remains the main point of reference for the spice, along with the flavouring of alcohol, from French pastis to Italian sambuca, mulled wine and mulled cider.

Such occasional and marginal use doesn't do the spice justice. As is often the way, going back to source is the best way to become inspired. Throughout South East Asia, star anise is often used to cut through strongly flavoured and fatty meat – as with braised pork belly or North-west China's Lanzhou beef noodle soup. It has the same effect when a seedpod is added to braised brisket, beef cheeks, oxtail or venison stew.

The anise notes work well in certain seafood dishes – it elevates fennel, celery and bay in a hearty bouillabaisse, or mussels cooked with a splash of Pernod. In sweeter contexts, a whole star anise might be used when making masala chai or Thai iced tea, poaching rhubarb, pears, plums (see Star Anise Roasted Plum and Yoghurt Cream Pavlova, page 202) and dried fruit winter compotes. It may even be used for a marmalade and star anise ice cream.

Perhaps the quickest way to incorporate it into everyday cooking is to pop a seedpod into an electric grinder, and get into the habit of stirring a little through buttery leeks or caramelised onions, over roasted sweet potato or into plum crumble or cherry cobbler. Star not just in name, but also in its ability to be the stardust that turns a simple dish into something a bit special.

Note

For a basic Chinese five spice recipe, toast equal amounts of star anise, cinnamon, cloves, fennel and Szechuan peppercorns in a dry frying pan (skillet) over a gentle heat until aromatic. Quickly cool, grind, sieve (strain) and store in an airtight container.

Sumac

Sumac is the splash of crimson-coloured spice that tops dishes throughout the Middle East. It's been described as a 'red thread' woven throughout the region, uniting dishes with a distinctive, tangy top note. It's used as a finishing flavour and a souring agent – a way to brighten and enhance the flavours on the plate, bringing them into sharper focus.

It's harvested from the sumac tree (which is in the Anacardiaceae family – the same as mangoes, pistachios and cashews). In early autumn (fall), cone-shaped bursts of tiny white flowers give way to small berry-like clusters. Botanically speaking, they're 'drupes' (not berries) – the term for thin-skinned, fleshy fruit with a central stone (pit), like cherries or apricots. They're harvested before the flesh has a chance to fully ripen, and are then sun-dried and ground into a fluffy powder, which typically has a high enough water content to take on a velvety sheen.

Sumac trees are becoming a more regular sight throughout Europe, but it's often North American Staghorn sumac that is planted in gardens. It's not this (typically ornamental) variety that produces the Middle Eastern spice, although a Native American recipe for 'sumac lemonade' (a tangy pink drink made by crushing and soaking drupes in water) is experiencing something of a revival thanks to foragers* keen to find edible inspiration close to home.

Instead, it is Sicilian sumac (known botanically as *Rhus coriaria*, or tanner's sumac) that is grown for the culinary spice. There's some irony surrounding its name, given the strong associations sumac has with the Middle East, not southern Italy. It's thought that sumac trees were first introduced to Sicily as far back as the 9th century, when Arab settlers realised they would thrive in the arid, rocky terrain.

Right up to the late-14th century, the spice was used as a way to bring acidity to a dish (the Tuscan cookbook *Libro della Cocina* contains a recipe for quails cooked in a ground almond and sumac sauce). It's no coincidence that the waning use of sumac coincided with the arrival of lemons. By the mid-15th century, lemons were cultivated in Liguria, and as the popularity of citrus fruit boomed, sumac disappeared from Italian cookbooks.

It's certainly not the case in the Middle East. While sumac is most often used in small pinches as a finishing flavour, it's occasionally nudged into the limelight – for example, the Palestinian dish

*There is a poisonous sumac tree (*Toxicodendron vernix*) – so a word of warning to keen foragers to carefully consult a botanical handbook before mixing up a batch of sumac lemonade.

msakhan, in which sweet onions seasoned with generous amounts (usually several tablespoons) of sumac are heaped on to flatbread and topped with chicken and pine nuts. In terms of daily use, sumac is used to season hummus, fattoush salads and barbecued meat, and is stirred through jewelled rice. It's also a key component in the Middle Eastern blend za'atar.

Sumac's brightness has made it a popular fusion ingredient that is easily adaptable. Think of it as a spicy squeeze of lemon that works particularly well in summer dishes. It's great with seafood: fried squid, barbecued prawns (shrimp) and fish, and works equally well as a rub or seasoning (see page 122 for Blackened Sumac Salmon Grain Bowls with Tahini Dressing). A drizzle of lemon-sumac vinaigrette is a light and summery way to dress runner beans and charred broccoli, while a pinch of sumac and chilli over pineapple or melon wedges brings delicious spiciness to delightfully balmy days.

Tomatoes with olive oil, salt and sumac

Olive oil with za'atar

Szechuan Peppercorns

Szechuan peppercorns are relatively new to Brits' spice racks. Their emergence fits with the swift evolution of our understanding of 'Chinese' cooking. In a single generation, there's been a shift from buffet tables heaving under the weight of sweet and sour orange-sauced dishes to a surging interest in regional cuisine – with all the specific ingredients, nuances and variation you'd expect from a country of 1.4 billion people.

Within China's 'eight culinary traditions' it's Szechuan (also 'Sichuan') cuisine, from China's south-western province, which is perhaps the best known. Its capital, Chengdu, was chosen as UNESCO's second ever 'City of Gastronomy' and the region's dishes are famed for their hot and numbing '*málà*'(麻辣) flavour profile. Chillies provide the spicy '*la*' but it's Szechuan peppercorns which bring the numbing '*ma*'– that distinctive lip-tingling sensation associated with mapo tofu, dandan noodles and Szechuan hotpot.

Misleadingly, Szechuan peppercorns are not, in fact, peppercorns, but berries from the prickly ash tree. They darken over the summer, hardening and then bursting open – sometimes popping in half into a teeny Pac-Man shape, and other times peeling open like a lotus flower, with a petal-like form. Harvesting the berries is labour-intensive, involving first picking around thorned branches, and then hand-sifting out dried stalks and twigs.

The reward is bagfuls of rough russet-red husks, which have grapefruit citrus notes when ground and create a fantastically tingly sensation – somewhere between spearmint, sherbet and a tiny electric current. This is down to a chemical compound (hydroxy-alpha sanshool), which causes micro-vibrations across the lips and tongue. The effect is almost cooling. It's said to help with Szechuan's endemic humidity and the walloping chilli heat that laces so many of the province's dishes.

Most often, Szechuan peppercorns are bought whole, lightly toasted and then ground in a pestle and mortar. They are often infused in oil, too – something that is done both on an industrial scale (bottles of pre-infused oil are widely available) and also by home cooks, who allow Szechuan peppercorns to crackle in a few tablespoons of neutral oil to impart their flavour, before flicking them out and commencing with a recipe.

The most straightforward way to start cooking more with Szechuan peppercorns is to grind the berries and simply use the resulting

Did you know?
There's an emerging body of recipe development aimed specifically at ageusia sufferers – in which taste is altered or altogether lost, perhaps due to the longterm effects of COVID-19 or chemotherapy (see *Life Kitchen* by Ryan Riley). Szechuan peppercorns present themselves as an interesting ingredient, thanks to their ability to add texture and an extra dimension to dishes.

Did you know?
Nepal's timut (timur) peppercorns and Japan's sansho (sansyo) peppercorns are both closely related to the Szechuan peppercorn, and are grown on shrubs in the prickly ash family.

powder as a seasoning alongside recipes with a Chinese flavour – scattering a pinch over noodle and rice dishes or smacked cucumbers (page 170). If tossing green beans or prawns (shrimp) with a little toasted sesame oil, ginger and spring onions (scallions), then get into the habit of reaching for Szechuan peppercorns over black peppercorns as a finishing flavour; this will only enhance and add an exciting top note.

It's little surprise that Szechuan peppercorns have been enthusiastically adopted by fusion cooks – the potential for experimentation is vast. Citrus notes allow them to straddle the savoury-sweet divide, meaning that they occasionally crop up in recipes for caramelised pineapple, pear tarte tatin and biscuits (cookies), like the Grapefruit and Szechuan Ricciarelli on page 188. Grinding the peppercorns with either salt or sugar gives further context to a Szechuan seasoning, and will help turn any thoughts of intimidation to sheer intrepidness when it comes to harnessing and embracing their electric power.

Turmeric

India's native turmeric transcends the spice rack. Its use is devotional, ritualistic: holy ceremonies, childbirth, weddings, funerals. Recently pierced ears? Rub turmeric paste on the lobe. Runny nose? Sip hot turmeric milk. Breakout of spots? Try a turmeric facemask.

The love for turmeric extends to kitchens up and down India. Not just for the bright yellow colour it imparts, but also its astringent pepperiness and floral top notes. India is the biggest grower, consumer and exporter (accounting for 80 per cent of global production), and throughout the country, it's rarer to come across a dish that doesn't contain turmeric than one that does.

The biggest farms are based in the south (Andhra Pradesh, Tamil Nadu and Karnataka) and West Bengal. Leaves sprout above ground, but it's all about the fist-sized rhizome below ground and the 'fingers' that grow off it, which are knobbly, like those of its fiery cousin, ginger. Once the turmeric fingers are harvested, they're boiled, peeled, polished and then dried in the sun for a couple of weeks, before being (mechanically) ground into a super-fine powder.

The biggest differential in types of turmeric comes from the soil in which it's grown. Plants thrive in red soil or clay loam, and Alleppey (on the south-western coast) has become a renowned growing region. It's famed for producing turmeric with a particularly high percentage of curcumin (6.5 per cent, versus the standard 3 per cent) – which is not only linked to the bright yellow colour, but a growing body of scientific research reinforces the ancient belief in its antiseptic and anti-inflammatory powers. The higher the curcumin, the higher the price.

Little surprise, then, that turmeric is celebrated in Alleppey's famous fish curry; in fact, it's the backbone of most Indian curries. Throughout India, it's not uncommon to be ingesting turmeric in some shape or form from morning to night – starting with *akuri* breakfast eggs or the masala filling of a dosa pancake, and then rounding off dinner with turmeric mango *kulfi* ice cream or *haldi doodh* (golden milk). It's said that 'white food' is such a turn-off, that turmeric is swirled through yoghurt sauces and mixed in oil for frying cauliflower, purely to take the edge off and impart a more desirable golden hue.

As with all spices, the movement of people is one of the primary ways that turmeric travelled further afield. Notably, when half a million Indian nationals settled across the Caribbean between 1838 and 1917, they inspired dishes such as curried chicken and stuffed rotis.

There's turmeric in the pastry of Jamaica's patties, and in Grenada's 'oil down' (meat and vegetable stew). In Indonesia, Malaysia and Singapore, turmeric is used in laksa, spiced rice and fried fish. As it was traded west through North Africa, it became a lead component in ras el hanout and *hawayej,* a Yemeni spice blend, and it is responsible for the beautiful yellow hue of *sfouf* – a Lebanese almond and turmeric cake.

Interestingly, there's almost no heritage of turmeric in Europe's cuisine beyond using it to colour winter butter (when the colour is pale from cows' hay-based diet), margarine, cheese, mustards and, of course, piccalilli. It's probably its inferior use as a dye that meant turmeric was dubbed 'poor man's saffron'. Certainly as a cooking ingredient, it rarely featured beyond curry powders, which is probably why Elizabeth David wrote in 1970: 'One ounce [30g] of turmeric is more than enough to buy at one time – unless you live off spiced rice and curries.'

The same certainly can't be said today. With more people than ever interested in holistic nutrition, turmeric has been nudged into the limelight. The culinary creativity that defines the movement has repositioned it in the kitchen: these days, turmeric colours poached eggs, homemade hummus, as well as the recipe for Golden Milk Custard Tart on page 206. It's knocked back as a morning shot, sipped in smoothie form and licked in iced lollies (ice pops). It sits happily alongside other South Asian ingredients like ginger, coconut, lime and tamarind (see Carrot, Turmeric and Tamarind Soup, page 126). An ounce disappears quickly in kitchens today.

Cynics might suggest that its colour is singularly exploited to beautify a dish, though the flavour of a good-quality turmeric is just as attractive. Deceptively, turmeric's yellow hue lasts for years, but its fragrance ebbs away far faster – the bright, peppery notes give way to a duller astringency. A sniff should reveal where it is in its life cycle. More than with any other spice, it's best to buy frequently and replenish stocks, rather than revive an old turmeric, to make sure that its flavour is as beautiful and bright as its colour.

Za'atar

This Middle Eastern blend is propped up by three core ingredients: Biblical hyssop, sesame seeds and sumac. The ratios vary from region to region. Typically, blends from Jordan contain more sumac, while Palestinian varieties have a bigger percentage of milled, green hyssop leaves. Sometimes the sesame is toasted, other times it's raw. Even within small localities, families have their own distinct blends – a closely guarded recipe handed down from one generation to the next.

Differences aside, the za'atar used throughout the Middle East is rich with heady, herbal aromas from the hyssop base. It's milled from slightly fuzzy heart-shaped leaves and has an almost fluffy texture to it. It's rare for a producer to be put out by a discrepancy in the ingredient ratios, but many have been appalled to see what's stocked in British supermarkets under the label 'za'atar': twiggy, dry spice mixes laced with cumin, wheat and citric acid.

Throughout the Middle East, small-scale za'atar production once fell within the natural rhythms of the year. In spring, wild mountain hyssop was picked and bunches were dried on patios and rooftops in the early summer sun. Now the crop is cultivated to cater for a growing demand, and many families' efforts have shifted from home production to tracking down the best supply. Sourcing trips have been steered by tip-offs on a 'blue door' down an alleyway, behind which the best za'atar blend in the city is sold, only to those in the know.

Throughout za'atar-loving regions, it's rare to find a meal untouched by the spice blend. It's sprinkled over breakfast labneh (strained yoghurt), mixed with oil for dunking bread into, brushed over pizza-like flatbreads (*manakish*) and used as a flavoursome crust to coat soft cheese (*shanklish*). As the spice blend travelled further afield, inspired chefs have introduced new aromatics: dried rose petals, fig leaf, orange peel, sage – even ground almonds and chopped pistachios (at which point, it arguably begins to merge more into a variant of the Egyptian nut-based spice blend, dukkah).

Even elaborate and embellished za'atar is best used in a familiar context. The herb base gives it a delicacy that works best with light flavours like fish (see Za'atar Fried Fish with Preserved Lemon Tartare, page 160) or chicken (see Za'atar Chicken Salad Sarnies, page 108) as well as soft cheeses, plain breads, and even pasta (see Tomato, Za'atar and Butter Pasta, page 127). The blend has a natural affinity with other Middle Eastern flavours – tomatoes, chickpeas (garbanzos), aubergines (eggplants) and regional grains (bulghur, couscous, freekeh). A small, well-timed pinch is often just enough to be transported to some of the most delicious corners of the world.

Did you know?
Most commonly, 'za'atar' refers to the name of the spice blend, but it's also the singular name of the herb that (confusingly) is also known as Biblical hyssop, Syrian oregano and wild thyme. It's in the mint family, and the main compound in za'atar leaves is carvacrol, which is also the main compound in oregano and thyme.

Golden Blend

Something happened around the 2010s. The most unexpected foods turned yellow. Between 2012 and 2016, there was a 300 per cent increase in online searches for 'turmeric' and nothing was safe: lattes, teas, tonics... dips, breads, eggs... cauliflower rice, smoothie bowls, nut cheeses.

Lots of people experimenting with pungent turmeric for the first time weren't impressed. As a singular, lead flavour (particularly when bitter, astringent turmeric is used) it's often quite unpalatable. After all, turmeric is more conventionally a background, earthy, bass note in a spice blend for more robust dishes like dhal, biryani or kedgeree – it's rarely a stand-alone spice.

That's how the idea of a 'golden blend' came about. Turmeric remains the lead flavour – and a yellow colour is still imparted – but sweet cinnamon and bright black pepper curb its abrasiveness. A pre-mixed tin means that small amounts can be used quickly in the modern contexts in which turmeric often finds itself: drop scones, homemade granola, scrambled tofu, spiced frittata, and so on.

This blend sings in dairy-based drinks and desserts that hark back to the cure-all Indian drink haldi doodh, in which turmeric is mixed with hot milk and sweetened with a little pinch of sugar. Its curative properties have long been recognised by Ayurvedic medicine – an ancient and holistic system still practised by 80 per cent of the population in India and Nepal – and it's been a source of much hilarity to Indian families to see haldi doodh sold in hip cafés, where it's rebranded as 'golden milk' or 'turmeric latte'.

Setting aside its alleged power as a superfood, and the discourse around its functionality in both ancient and 21st-century medicine, its flavour alone makes golden blend a beautiful and popular spice mix. It's nourishing when mixed into porridge (oatmeal) and phenomenal in a carrot cake – perhaps not traditional, but transformational.

Golden Blend ingredients

- 2 teaspoons ground turmeric
- ½ teaspoon ground cinnamon
- ¼ teaspoon finely ground black pepper

From a health perspective, there's evidence to suggest that adding black pepper to turmeric boosts the body's ability to absorb the beneficial curcumin from the turmeric.

House Blend

Rooted Spices' (Rachel's spice company) 'House Blend' was developed as an everyday alternative to salt and pepper: a 'Third Table Spice'. With the gentle heat from pul biber chillies (Aleppo and Urfa) and brightness from cured sumac there are few dishes it can't enliven and enhance. Its versatility make it perfect for adding to breakfast eggs, avocado toast and cream cheese bagels.

It's by no means a prescriptive spice blend, but more of a concept. 'Season with salt and pepper' is often given as an absent-minded instruction. Its ubiquity means that so many dishes which would benefit from a colourful final flourish are deprived of it. It's not the case in countries where spice blends are put out on café tables to encourage liberal use (such as with Mexico's *tajín* seasoning or Japan's shichimi togarashi).

If there's one takeaway from this book, then please make it the addition of an everyday seasoning beyond the standard salt and pepper. It hardly matters what. A large pestle and mortar sat atop the kitchen countertop makes a good receptacle for an ever-evolving 'house blend' of sorts. It might be dictated by mood, season and (more often than not) the dregs of a spice tin that need using up.

Currently, my mortar contains a mix of crushed coriander seeds, black peppercorns, fennel seeds, Aleppo pul biber and salt. It's recently been flung over hummus on toast, ratatouille with feta and spaghetti with a tomato and anchovy sauce. It's a pride-inducing exercise, seasoning a dish in such a carefree and creative fashion, and is the gateway to thinking more about using spices on a daily basis. It's not to say that there's no place for the peppermill, but use it in conjunction with your spice rack and you'll reap the benefits.

Note: for the sake of recipes in this book, the Rooted Spices 'House Blend' has been used (guide recipe right), although any personal variation may be used as a substitute.

House Blend ingredients

- 2 tablespoons Aleppo chilli pepper
- 1 tablespoon Urfa chilli pepper
- 1 teaspoon ground sumac

Tips on making your own House Blend

- Avoid any spices that are too potent (cumin, cayenne pepper, star anise).

- Be conscious that using sweet spices (cinnamon) might limit its uses in an everyday, savoury context.

- If you're using chillies, then best to start with something mild – going too hot can be divisive, makes it less versatile and can overpower a dish. Turkish pul biber chillies or a Mexican ancho are both great options.

- Don't make up too much house blend in one go. Spices start to lose their potency as soon as they're ground. The quantities in the above recipe are a good place to start.

- Getting a small, lidded pinch pot to sit alongside the salt and pepper grinder is a good idea, and will help keep a house blend more potent by protecting it from the elements.

Breakfast and Brunch

Warm Cinnamon Granola Scones with Whipped Honey Butter

Cinnamon (page 34)

Makes 6

Takes: 50 mins
Effort level: Easy

- 250 g (9 oz/2 cups) self-raising (self-rising) flour, plus extra for dusting
- ¼ teaspoon sea salt
- 1 heaped tablespoon ground cinnamon
- 70 g (2½ oz) cold unsalted butter, cubed
- 30 g (1 oz/3¾ tablespoons) caster (superfine) sugar
- 50 g (2 oz) granola, plus a handful for sprinkling (use a nuttier rather than fruitier version)
- 150 ml (5 fl oz/⅔ cup) full-fat (whole) milk
- 1 egg, beaten

For the whipped honey butter
- 100 g (3½ oz) unsalted butter, softened
- 50 g (2 oz/2¾ tablespoons) runny honey
- good pinch of sea salt

Scones are such an easy thing to throw together when you have people popping over or are in need of a sweet treat. They require little skill and inexpensive ingredients. There's something welcoming about these cinnamon-flavoured scones first thing in the morning, eating them while still warm and slathered in honey butter, although they can be enjoyed any time of the day, of course.

1. Preheat the oven to 180°C fan (350°F/gas 6) and line a baking sheet with baking parchment.

2. Sift the flour, salt and cinnamon into a large bowl. Add the butter and rub it in with your fingers until it's a fine, breadcrumb-like mixture. Stir through the sugar and granola, then quickly stir in the milk, combining it with a cutlery knife. Turn the mixture out on to a lightly floured work surface and knead until it just comes together (don't be tempted to overknead, or you'll be left with a tough dough). Shape into a 17 cm (6½ in) round disc and cut into 6 triangles.

3. Arrange the scones on the prepared baking sheet, brush with the beaten egg and sprinkle with some extra granola. Bake for 15–18 minutes until golden brown. Leave to cool for 5 minutes.

4. For the honey butter, using electric hand-held beaters or a stand mixer fitted with a whisk attachment, beat the butter, honey and sea salt together at a high speed for 5 minutes, or until lightly whipped. Cut open the warm scones and spread with the honey butter. Store any leftover scones in an airtight container for up to 3 days.

Extra ideas

- The honey butter will keep in the refrigerator for up to a week and frozen for 3 months. Try melting it on hot crumpets, pancakes or waffles.
- Add 1–2 teaspoons ground cinnamon to a chilli con carne or to the Slow-cooked Ancho Beef Shin on page 137 to crank it up a notch.
- Whip cinnamon, sugar and cream together and serve with stewed plums or ripe figs on top of a pavlova.
- Add cinnamon to your favourite blondie recipe with pecans and dried slices of apple or pears.

Mango, Coconut and Cardamom Bircher Muesli

Cardamom (page 28)

Serves 4

Takes: 10 mins, plus overnight soaking
Effort level: Easy

- 2 large ripe mangoes or 1 × 400 g (14 oz) can mango pulp
- 1 large apple, coarsely grated
- 150 g (5 oz/1½ cups) rolled oats
- 50 g (2 oz/½ cup) desiccated (dried shredded) coconut
- 50 g (2 oz/2¾ tablespoons) runny honey
- 5 cardamom pods, pods split open and seeds crushed
- 200 g (7 oz) Greek or coconut yoghurt
- 200 ml (7 fl oz/scant ½ cup) milk (dairy or plant-based both work well)
- finely grated zest and juice of 1 lime, plus extra grated lime zest to serve
- 50 g (2 oz/⅓ cup) toasted pistachios, chopped

The Swiss breakfast of Bircher is very simple – just soak oats with milk, dried fruits and nuts. You can make lots of different versions too. This one has an almost mango lassi-esque flavour, with puréed mango, coconut yoghurt and the herbal warmth of cardamom.

1. Peel, stone (pit) and slice the mangoes, then whizz half the mango in a food processor to form a smooth purée. Cover the rest and chill in the refrigerator for the next day.

2. Mix the puréed mango with the apple, oats, coconut, honey, cardamom, yoghurt, milk, lime juice and grated zest in a large bowl. Cover and leave to chill in the refrigerator overnight to become thick and creamy.

3. Serve the next day in bowls topped with the remaining sliced mango, extra grated lime zest and toasted pistachios. This will keep, chilled, for up to 2 days.

Extra ideas

- **Cinnamon, apple and pear Bircher muesli** – Add an extra apple to the mix instead of the mango. Swap the coconut and pistachios for mixed seeds and nuts, use plain yoghurt, swap the cardamom for 1 tablespoon ground cinnamon and swap the lime for lemon.
- **Cardamom and apple flapjacks** – Preheat the oven to 140°C fan (280°F/gas 3). Grease and line a 20 × 20 cm (8 × 8 in) square baking tin (pan) with baking parchment. Tip 200 g (7 oz) salted butter, 200 g (7 oz/½ cup) golden (light corn) syrup and 200 g (7 oz/1 cup) soft brown sugar into a saucepan. Stir for 5 minutes, or until the butter has melted and the sugar has dissolved. Tip 350 g (12 oz/3½ cups) rolled oats into a large bowl with 1 grated apple, the ground seeds of 7 cardamom pods, 1 teaspoon ground cinnamon, 50 g (2 oz/scant ½ cup) chopped hazelnuts and 50 g (2 oz/scant ½ cup) sultanas (golden raisins). Stir in the butter mix. Spoon the mixture into the prepared tin and press down with the back of a spoon. Bake for 35 minutes. Leave to cool in the tin completely.

Cardamom-poached Apricots

Cardamom (page 28)

Serves 4

Takes: 25 mins
Effort level: Easy

- 100 g (3 ½ oz/scant ½ cup) golden caster (superfine) sugar
- 7 cardamom pods, lightly bashed
- 300 ml (10 fl oz/1¼ cups) water
- 500 g (1 lb 2 oz) ripe apricots, halved and stoned (pitted)
- juice of 1 lemon

There are a few better ways to celebrate the start of summer than poaching the first of the apricots. Adding a few crushed cardamom pods is such an easy way to introduce floral, fragrant top notes and take things to the next level.

A large jar of poached apricots will keep in the refrigerator for a few days, and is a treat to delve into at breakfast – try adding to yoghurt and granola. If, in the unlikely event, you have some left after a few days, then blitz the soft apricots with a little of the syrup and serve with Prosecco for cardamom apricot-scented Bellinis.

1. Heat the sugar and cardamom in a medium saucepan over a medium heat. Pour in the water and stir until the sugar has dissolved. Add the apricots, then reduce the heat to low and poach gently for 10–15 minutes until tender.

2. Leave the apricots and poaching liquor to cool completely, then stir through the lemon juice. Tip into a clean 1 litre (34 fl oz) jar, seal and leave in the refrigerator for up to a week.

Extra ideas

- **Apricot frangipane** – Apricot and cardamom is a classic flavour pairing that works so well in summer bakes. Stir a few ground cardamom seeds in with the ground almonds when making an almond sponge or frangipane tart, then push a few of the poached apricots into the top before baking.
- Stone fruits and cardamom work particularly well together, such as in the Creamy Rice Pudding with Cardamom Peaches recipe (page 204).

Sausage Sarnies with Sticky Ras el Hanout Onions

Chillies (page 32) **Fennel Seeds** (page 42) **Ras el Hanout** (page 64)

Serves 4

Takes: 40 mins
Effort level: Easy

- 40 g (1½ oz) unsalted butter
- 1 tablespoon olive oil
- 5 red or brown onions, thinly sliced
- 1 tablespoon ras el hanout
- 1 teaspoon fennel seeds, crushed
- pinch of chilli (hot pepper) flakes
- 1 teaspoon soft brown sugar
- 8 pork sausages
- sea salt

To serve
- 8 thick slices of white bread or 4 large crusty baps
- butter
- mustard

Ras el hanout is a versatile spice mix that can really pack a punch. With a blend ranging from the earthiness of cumin to the sweetness of cinnamon, cardamom and fennel, it works well with red meat. Here, it's cooked slowly with onions and paired with fat pork sausages: a classic combination that has been given a spicy modern twist, elevating it for the better.

1. Heat the butter and oil in a saucepan over a low–medium heat. Add the onions and a pinch of salt and cook for 20 minutes, or until softened, golden and sticky. Add the ras el hanout, fennel, chilli and sugar and cook for a further 2 minutes. Taste for seasoning, adding a little more salt if you feel it needs it.

2. Fry the sausages in a large frying pan (skillet) over a medium heat for 10–12 minutes until cooked through and golden brown, then remove from the pan and halve them lengthways.

3. To serve, spread the bread or baps with the butter and mustard, then top with the sausages and sticky onions and sandwich together. Alternatively, serve the ras el hanout onions at a barbecue with sausages and burgers.

Extra ideas

- Try roasting red onion wedges with the ras el hanout and serving them on flatbreads topped with tahini sauce or hummus.
- Melt some butter and ras el hanout together, then swirl it through plain yoghurt with a pinch of salt for an easy dip.
- Use ras el hanout to marinate meat and fish before grilling (broiling).

Spice Breakfast Lassi

Cumin (page 40), **Fennel Seeds** (page 42),
Golden Blend (page 80) or **Turmeric** (Page 76)

Serves 1

Takes: 10 mins
Effort level: Easy

- ¼ teaspoon cumin seeds, plus extra for sprinkling
- ¼ teaspoon fennel seeds
- 1 ripe banana or the chopped flesh of 1 small, ripe mango
- ½ teaspoon Golden Blend (page 80) or turmeric (optional)
- 100 g (3½ oz/scant ½ cup) full-fat (whole) natural yoghurt (dairy or plant-based)
- 100 ml (3½ fl oz/scant ½ cup) milk (dairy or plant-based)
- 2 ice cubes
- 25 g (1 oz/¼ cup) rolled or porridge oats
- 1–2 tablespoons honey

Lassi originated in India. It's a creamy yoghurt drink that is either sweetened or salted and sometimes blended with mango, pistachio or rose water, and flavoured with toasted cumin or fennel seeds. This is a recipe of sorts, but really it's a base idea. You can swap the fruit around to your liking, adding mango or raspberries instead of banana. But make sure you keep the toasted spices, as they really crank up the flavour and make it something special.

1. Toast the cumin and fennel seeds in a dry frying pan (skillet) over a low heat for 5 minutes. Remove the pan from the heat and leave to cool slightly.

2. Tip the banana, toasted spices, Golden Blend or turmeric, yoghurt, milk, ice cubes, oats and honey into a high-speed blender and blend until smooth. Pour into a tall glass and sprinkle with some extra cumin seeds.

Extra ideas

- Add toasted cumin seeds to finish the Mango, Coconut and Cardamom Bircher Muesli on page 86.
- Stir 1–2 teaspoons Golden Blend into your porridge as it's cooking or into Bircher Muesli. Particularly delicious when sweetened with soaked sultanas (golden raisins) or honey.

Spice Rack Cured Salmon

Coriander Seeds (page 36), **Fennel Seeds** (page 42), **Ginger** (page 48) or **Peppercorns** (Page 58)

Makes 1 × 800 g (1 lb 12 oz) piece
Serves 6–8

Takes: 30 mins, plus 48 hrs chilling
Effort level: Easy

- 800 g (1 lb 12 oz) piece of salmon or trout, the best quality you can find, skin on
- 1 tablespoon fennel seeds
- 1 tablespoon coriander seeds
- 1½ tablespoons ground ginger
- 1 teaspoon black peppercorns
- 70 g (2½ oz/½ cup) sea salt flakes
- 50 g (2 oz/¼ cup) soft light brown sugar
- finely grated zest of 1 lemon
- 3 tablespoons gin or vodka

To serve (optional)
- crispbreads or rye bread
- crème fraîche
- Deli Pickles (page 178)

Curing salmon gravlax-style under a salt and sugar blanket is relatively simple. Once the salt mix and spices encase the fish, all it takes is several days of waiting and you're left with something impressive and satisfying. You can play around with the spices in this recipe to suit whatever you have on your spice rack, or adjust the quantities for your palate (see below for more ideas). The salmon can be thinly sliced and eaten on rye bread or bagels with sour cream, and is great on blinis at Christmas.

1. Lay the salmon skin-side down on a rimmed baking sheet. Check the salmon for bones by running your fingers down the centre and pulling any out you can find with tweezers.

2. Heat a small frying pan (skillet) over a medium heat, then add the spices and toast for 3 minutes. Set aside to cool slightly, then grind the spices in a spice grinder or pestle and mortar to a coarse texture. Tip them into a bowl with the salt, sugar, lemon zest and gin or vodka and mix together, then pack the mix tightly over the salmon. Cover with cling film (plastic wrap) and leave to chill in the refrigerator for 24 hours. After this time, flip the salmon over and chill for a further 12–24 hours.

3. Once the salmon is cured, brush off most of the cure and discard.

4. Lay the salmon on a serving board and slice into thin slices. Serve with crispbreads or rye bread, crème fraîche and Deli Pickles, if you like.

Try these other flavour combinations

- 1 tablespoon fennel seeds + ½ tablespoon black peppercorns + finely grated zest of 1 large orange.
- ½ tablespoon ancho chilli powder + 2 tablespoons coriander seeds + finely grated zest of 2 limes.
- 1 tablespoon juniper berries + finely grated zest of 1 grapefruit + 1 tablespoon black peppercorns.
- 2 tablespoons za'atar + ½ tablespoon Urfa chilli (hot pepper) pepper flakes + 1 tablespoon coriander seeds + 2 chopped preserved lemons.

Turkish Eggs (Çılbır)

Pul Biber (page 60)

Serves 2

Takes: 15 mins
Effort level: Easy

- 300 g (10½ oz) full-fat (whole) thick Greek yoghurt
- 1 small garlic clove, finely grated
- ¼ teaspoon sea salt flakes, plus extra to season
- 40 g (1½ oz) unsalted butter
- 1 teaspoon Aleppo chilli pepper
- 1 tablespoon white wine vinegar
- 4 cold eggs
- handful of dill, torn
- handful of parsley, torn
- toasted sourdough, to serve

Turkish eggs (*çılbır*) is a dish that needs to be shouted about and celebrated in as many cookbooks as possible, because it is truly exceptional. Dating back to the 15th century in the Ottoman Empire, poached eggs sit on a bed of thick, creamy, garlicky yoghurt before being drizzled with warm chilli butter. You'd never have guessed that the combination of a poached egg and yoghurt would be so good, but paired with a chilli-spiked butter and a crunchy hunk of toast, this makes one of the best egg dishes around, and you should cook it, order it and talk about it for as long as you can.

1. Mix the yoghurt, garlic and sea salt together in a large bowl. Chill in the refrigerator until needed.

2. Heat the butter in a large frying pan (skillet) over a medium heat until foaming, then add the Aleppo chilli pepper and fry for 2 minutes. Add a pinch of salt. Set aside.

3. Bring a deep saucepan of salted water to a simmer. Coat an egg cup or small ramekin (custard cup) with some of the vinegar, then crack an egg into the cup. Reduce the heat to a very low simmer and swirl the water vigorously to create a vortex. When the vortex has almost subsided, carefully drop the egg into it. Cook for 3 minutes, undisturbed, then carefully scoop out the egg with a slotted spoon and set aside on a plate. Repeat with the remaining eggs.

4. Warm the butter. Spoon the yoghurt into 4 bowls, then top with the eggs, spiced butter and herbs. Serve with lots of thick, toasted sourdough for dunking.

Extra ideas

- **Aleppo butter corn** – Mix 1 tablespoon Aleppo chilli pepper with 80 g (3 oz) unsalted butter, 30 g (1 oz) grated Parmesan or vegetarian hard cheese and a pinch of salt. Par-boil 6 corn-on-the-cobs for 10 minutes, then grill (broil) or griddle for 10 minutes and turn a few times, until lightly charred and brush with the butter.
- **Aleppo fried eggs** – In a large frying pan (skillet), fry the eggs in oil over a high heat until crispy, then sprinkle with Aleppo chilli pepper and lots of salt.

Macerated Strawberries with Fennel Seeds

Fennel Seeds (page 42)

Serves 4

Takes: 10 mins, plus
1 hr macerating
Effort level: Easy

- 400 g (14 oz) strawberries, hulled and sliced
- finely grated zest and juice of 1 lemon
- 1½ teaspoons fennel seeds, crushed
- 50 g (2 oz/scant ¼ cup) caster (superfine) sugar
- granola, thick Greek yoghurt, ice cream or whipped cream, to serve

Don't be put off by the combination of fennel seeds and berries; these strawberries take on a whole new flavour when macerated in the liquorice-like fennel, and are very moreish. They are great served at breakfast with yoghurt and granola, or in summer with cold cream or spooned on top of a pavlova. They are also very special blitzed and churned into the Strawberry and Fennel Seed Ice Cream on page 197.

1. Tip the strawberries into a large bowl, squeeze over the lemon juice and stir through the fennel seeds and sugar. Leave to stand for at least 1 hour, or overnight in the refrigerator.

2. Serve with granola, thick Greek yoghurt, ice cream or whipped cream.

Extra ideas

- Try baking a Victoria sponge, then piling the macerated strawberries between the layers and sandwiching everything together with sweetened whipped cream.
- Fennel seeds work beautifully with white chocolate; try adding 1 teaspoon fennel seeds to a white chocolate cookie or shortbread recipe.

Chana Masala Baked Eggs

Amchur (page 26), **Chilli** (page 32), **Cumin** (page 40), **Coriander Seeds** (page 36)
Garam Masala (page 44), **Ginger** (page 48), **Turmeric** (page 76)

Serves 2

Takes: 30 mins
Effort level: Easy

- 1 tablespoon rapeseed (canola) or vegetable oil
- 1 tablespoon ghee or unsalted butter
- 1 small onion, finely chopped
- 5 cm (2 in) piece of fresh ginger root, peeled and grated
- 2 garlic cloves, grated
- 2 teaspoons cumin seeds
- 2 teaspoons ground coriander or crushed coriander seeds
- ½ teaspoon Kashmiri or mild chilli powder
- ½ teaspoon ground turmeric
- 2 teaspoons amchur powder
- 400 g (14 oz) tin chopped tomatoes, blended in a food processor or with a hand-held blender
- 1 small green chilli, halved
- 750 g (1 lb 10 oz) jar giant chickpeas or 2 × 400 g (14 oz) tins chickpeas (garbanzos), reserve the jar or tin liquid
- 1 teaspoon sea salt
- 2 teaspoons garam masala
- 4 eggs
- ½ small red onion, very finely chopped
- ½ bunch of coriander (cilantro), finely chopped
- chapati or roti, to serve

Chana masala is a dish that plays host to some of the most cherished spices from the Indian subcontinent, namely cumin seeds, turmeric, garam masala and the dried mango powder amchur.

Chickpeas (garbanzos) take centre stage in this richly spiced tomato-based dish. It is very easy to throw together. The amchur transforms it, giving it a slightly fruity acidity. Adding eggs makes it a delicious dish for brunch or a speedy midweek dinner. Serve it with a chapati to scoop up the delicious spiced sauce.

1. Melt the oil and ghee in a shallow casserole dish (Dutch oven) or deep frying pan (skillet) over a low-medium heat. Add the onion and fry for 10–12 minutes until softened and translucent. Add the ginger and garlic and cook for 1 minute, then stir through the cumin, coriander, chilli, turmeric and amchur and fry for a further 1 minute. Add the tomatoes, chilli and chickpeas and their liquid, then bring to a simmer and cook, uncovered, over a low heat for 15 minutes, stirring frequently until thickened and saucy. Season with the salt and garam masala.

2. Make 4 wells in the chickpeas and crack an egg into each one. Cover with a lid and cook over a low heat for 5–7 minutes until the eggs are set and the yolks runny.

3. Top with the red onion and coriander and serve with bread for dunking.

Quick tips

- Look out for Indian dishes that require amchur, such as pav bhaji, bhindi bhaji and chole to name a few.
- Add ½ teaspoon amchur to a smoothie for a fruity sourness and additional vitamin C.

Weeknight Supper

Crispy Veg Fritters and Kachumber Salad

Cumin (page 40), **Coriander** (page 36), **Paprika** (page 56)

Serves 4 (makes 8 fritters)

Takes: 35 mins
Effort level: Easy

- 2 teaspoons ground cumin
- 2 teaspoons ground coriander
- 1½ teaspoons hot smoked paprika
- ½ cauliflower, roughly chopped, including leaves
- ½ onion, coarsely grated
- 1 carrot, coarsely grated
- 200 g (7 oz) tin sweetcorn, drained
- 1 teaspoon sea salt
- 200 g (7 oz/generous 1¾ cups) chickpea (gram) flour
- 150 ml (5 fl oz/⅔ cup) water
- vegetable or sunflower oil, for frying
- yoghurt of choice or Green Yoghurt (page 119), to serve

For the kachumber
- 2 teaspoons cumin seeds
- 200 g (7 oz) cherry tomatoes, halved
- ½ small red onion, roughly chopped
- ½ large cucumber, roughly chopped
- ½ bunch of mint or coriander (cilantro), roughly chopped
- juice of 1 lemon, plus extra to serve
- ½ teaspoon sea salt

These fritters are made using three of the most popular spices around – cumin, ground coriander and paprika. This is a sort of no-waste, clever vegan recipe to use up whatever vegetables you have in the refrigerator. The kachumber salad (an Indian salad of chopped tomatoes, onion and cucumber) accompanies the fried fritters perfectly with its fresh cumin seed crunch and lemony zing.

1. In a dry frying pan (skillet), lightly toast the cumin, coriander and paprika, then tip into a large bowl. Add the coarsely grated vegetables, the sweetcorn and salt. Add the flour and water and mix everything together well. Leave to chill in the refrigerator while you make the salad.

2. For the salad, lightly toast the cumin seeds in a dry frying pan, then tip these into a large bowl with the tomatoes, red onion, cucumber, mint or coriander, lemon juice and salt.

3. Preheat the oven to 100°C fan/210°F/gas ½ and line a large baking sheet with baking parchment. Heat 1 cm (½ in) of oil in a large frying pan over a medium-high heat. Drop 3 tablespoons of the batter into the pan to make one fritter and repeat. Fry the fritters in batches of 2–3 for 4 minutes on each side, or until deep golden brown and crispy, then set aside on the prepared baking sheet in the oven to keep warm.

4. Serve the fritters with the kachumber salad, yoghurt of choice and extra lemon to squeeze over. They are also delicious with a poached egg for a weekend brunch.

Extra ideas

- **Smoky paprika and rosemary sausage stew** – In a large saucepan, fry 1 chopped onion, 1 chopped celery stalk and 1 chopped carrot in 1 tablespoon olive oil over a low-medium heat for 10 minutes. Add 1 tablespoon smoked paprika and 1 crushed garlic clove and fry for 1 minute. Tip in 2 × 400 g (14 oz) tins chopped tomatoes, 2 × 400 g (14 oz) tins cannellini beans, 1 tablespoon red wine vinegar, 2 teaspoons caster (superfine) sugar and 1 tablespoon chopped rosemary. Bring to a simmer and cook, uncovered, for 20 minutes, stirring occasionally. Meanwhile, fry 8 meat or vegan sausages in a frying pan (skillet) over a medium heat for 7 minutes, or until golden brown. Add these to the stew, cover with a lid and cook for 10–15 minutes over a low-medium heat. Serve the stew with steamed green vegetables or polenta (cornmeal).

Creamy Tomato and Za'atar Soup

Za'atar (page 78)

Serves 4

Takes: 45 mins
Effort level: Easy

- 2 tablespoons olive oil, plus extra for drizzling
- 1 onion, finely chopped
- 3 celery stalks, chopped
- 1 garlic clove, crushed
- 3 tablespoons za'atar, plus extra to serve
- 3 × 400 g (14 oz) tins chopped tomatoes
- 1 tablespoon tomato purée (paste)
- 1 teaspoon caster (superfine) sugar
- 400 ml (13 fl oz/generous 1½ cups) full-fat (whole) milk
- 100 ml (3½ fl oz/scant ½ cup) double (heavy) cream
- sea salt
- cheese toasties or crusty bread and butter, to serve

This recipe is like a posh, revamped tinned tomato soup. If you have a quarter of a pot of za'atar lingering on your spice rack (it's best eaten sooner rather than later to retain its freshness!) then this is an easy way to use it: by creating the ultimate comfort dish. Za'atar and tomatoes love each other, and this storecupboard soup has a rich creaminess and zingy edge.

1. Heat the oil in a large saucepan or casserole dish (Dutch oven) over a medium heat. Add the onion and celery, along with a pinch of salt, and fry gently for 12–15 minutes until softened and the onion is translucent. Add the garlic and za'atar and cook for 1 minute. Stir through the tomatoes, tomato purée and sugar, then bring to a simmer, cover with a lid and cook for 30 minutes.

2. Blend the soup with a hand-held blender until smooth, then gently stir through the milk, cream and some salt to taste. Ladle into bowls and top with extra za'atar and a good drizzle of oil. Serve with gooey cheese toasties or crusty bread and butter.

Quick tips

- Za'atar is great stirred into all sort of soups to take them up a notch. Try it in lentil-based soups and sweet potato soup – or substitute – it for the coriander in a carrot-based one.
- Sprinkle za'atar on to cheese on toast for the final minute of grilling (broiling) or stir it into a Welsh rarebit mix – yum.

Za'atar Chicken Salad Sarnies

Za'atar (page 78)

Serves 4

Takes: 15 mins
Effort level: Easy

- 4 large roasted chicken thighs or 300 g (10½ oz) cooked leftover roast chicken
- ½ red onion or 2 spring onions (scallions), very finely chopped
- 1 celery stalk, very finely chopped
- 70 g (2½ oz/¼ cup) mayonnaise
- 70 g (2½ oz) sour cream or Greek yoghurt
- 2–4 teaspoons za'atar
- 8 thick slices of focaccia or soft sliced bread, white or wholemeal
- ½ butterhead or little gem lettuce, torn
- sea salt
- crisps (chips), to serve (yes, do it!)

A chicken salad sandwich can be really, really beautiful thing. It's all about having a balance of acidity in the dressing (achieved by adding sour cream or yoghurt) and that delicious crunch from the onion and very finely chopped celery. What makes a chicken salad even better is za'atar. With its citrussy, herby notes, it couldn't be a better friend for chicken. Start with 2 teaspoons and add more according to your taste, then pile it on to thick bread and eat it with salty crisps (chips) on the side, or squish them into the sandwich itself for extra crunch.

1. Using 2 forks, shred the cooked chicken, then roughly chop it. Tip the chicken into a large bowl, then add the onion, celery, mayonnaise, sour cream or yoghurt, za'atar and some salt, and mix everything together well. Check for seasoning, adding a little more salt if you feel it needs it.

2. Pile the chicken filling on to 4 sides of the bread, top with the torn lettuce, then add the remaining bread slices on top. Squish everything together, then halve the sandwiches and serve with crisps.

Extra ideas

- **Roast chicken with za'atar butter** – Preheat the oven to 200°C (400°F/ gas 7). Mix 70 g (2½ oz) salted butter with 2 tablespoons za'atar and stuff this under the skin of a whole medium chicken. Sprinkle the skin with sea salt flakes. Stuff half a lemon into the cavity and roast for 1 hour–1 hour 15 minutes until the chicken is golden and crispy and the flesh is cooked through. Don't waste the herby, buttery juices; spoon them over the carved chicken.
- Za'atar is great in other sandwiches – it's wonderful with good-quality tuna mayonnaise or mashed with yoghurt and feta to make a creamy spread.

Caraway Greens and Sausages

Caraway (page 27)

Serves 4

Takes: 35 mins
Effort level: Easy

- 20 g (¾ oz) unsalted butter
- 1 tablespoon olive oil
- 1 large onion, thinly sliced
- 1 teaspoon caraway seeds
- 1 pointed spring cabbage, sliced into 3 cm (1¼ in) ribbons
- 200 g (7 oz) spring greens, sliced into 3 cm (1¼ in) ribbons
- 400 ml (13 fl oz/generous 1½ cups) strong chicken stock
- ½ teaspoon cider vinegar
- 2 tablespoons crème fraîche
- 2 teaspoons Dijon mustard, plus extra to serve
- sea salt and freshly ground black pepper

To serve

- 8 cooked sausages (either good-quality British pork sausages or German bratwurst style)
- mashed or boiled potatoes

The rounded flavours of cabbage and greens work really well alongside the hearty, aromatic and slightly bitter taste of caraway seeds. Cabbage and caraway are often seen together in German, Hungarian and Austrian dishes. Traditional uses are in the fermented cabbage dish of sauerkraut, Hungarian goulash and often beetroot-based recipes. For this recipe, use a good-quality bratwurst or frankfurter sausage if you can; the smokier the better, as the saltier side to these sausages really elevates the nutty, bittersweet taste of the caraway seeds. Braising cabbage in this way gives you the added benefit of serving it straight from a warm pan at the dinner table rather than classically steaming or boiling it only for it to get cold and a little unpleasant on your plate!

1. Heat the butter and olive oil in a large, shallow casserole dish (Dutch oven) or lidded frying pan (skillet) over a low-medium heat. Add the onion and a good pinch of salt and fry gently for 15 minutes, or until golden. Add the caraway seeds and cook for 1 minute. Stir through the cabbage, spring greens, stock and a good pinch of sea salt. Cover with a lid and simmer gently for 7 minutes. Uncover and add the cider vinegar, crème fraîche and mustard. Simmer, uncovered, for a further 3 minutes. Season to taste with salt and pepper.

2. Serve the greens in shallow bowls topped with the sausages, potatoes and some extra mustard.

Extra ideas

- Caraway pairs extraordinarily well with onion. Try adding some caraway and caramelised onion to a soda bread, or add a pinch to a French onion soup or the base of an onion and potato pie.
- **Roasted roots with caraway butter** – Preheat the oven to 180°C fan (350°F/gas 6). Peel and dice 1 celeriac (celery root), then scrub and chop 3 parsnips and 3 carrots into chunky rounds. Tip the vegetables into a large saucepan of cold water, bring to the boil and cook for 4 minutes. Drain. Toss in a roasting tin (pan) with 1 quartered red onion, 3 bashed garlic cloves, 1 tablespoon olive oil, 1 tablespoon caraway seeds, 1 tablespoon chopped rosemary and some salt. Roast for 35–40 minutes, tossing twice while cooking. Add 1 tablespoon butter and toss to finish. Season to taste with salt.

Cacio e Pepe

Peppercorns (page 58)

Serves 2

Takes: 15 mins
Effort level: A little effort

- 2 teaspoons black peppercorns
- 90 g (31/4 oz) pecorino romano, at room temperature
- 230 g (8 oz) spaghetti or tonnarelli
- sea salt

One of the iconic trio of famous Roman pastas, alongside carbonara and gricia. Cacio e pepe, if you didn't already know, simply means 'cheese and pepper'. The cheese is pecorino and the pepper is coarsely ground black peppercorns. Traditionally, these two elements are tossed with tonnarelli (a thick spaghetti) and a good quantity of starchy cooking water. Follow these simple rules: don't overfill the pan with water; grind the cheese to a fine powder and turn it into a paste before using; and toss everything together off the heat – with practice, you will be able to recreate your favourite Roman holiday dish with ease.

1. Grind the peppercorns coarsely in a spice grinder or pestle and mortar. Add them to a large, deep, dry frying pan (skillet) and fry over a medium heat for 3 minutes. Remove from the heat and set aside.

2. Blitz the cheese in a food processor until it is a very fine, powdery texture. Tip into a large heatproof bowl and set aside.

3. Bring a large saucepan of lightly salted water to a simmer (don't overfill it – you want the pasta just submerged to make it as starchy as possible). Add the pasta and cook for 7 minutes for spaghetti or 9 minutes for tonnarelli. Five minutes before the end of cooking, scoop out 150ml (5 fl oz/⅔ cup) of the water. Leave to cool slightly, then mix 50 ml (1¾ fl oz/3 tablespoons) of this water with the cheese to make a paste.

4. Add the remaining 100 ml (3½ fl oz/scant 1½ cup) of the water to the pan with the pepper. Bring to a simmer and cook for 3–5 minutes until the water has reduced a little and is starchy. Add the pasta to the pan and toss everything together. Remove from the heat and leave to stand for 3 minutes, then tip the pasta into the cheese paste and toss everything together until you have a creamy sauce. Divide between 2 bowls and eat straight away.

Quick tip

- Pepper burns easily, so don't be tempted to use it when cooking over a high heat. Add as a finish to a steak rather than pre-cooking, or when browning chunks of meat for a stew, and only season with salt prior to frying it.

Khichdi with Spinach

Chilli (page 32), **Cumin** (page 40), **Coriander** (page 36), **Ginger** (page 48), **Mustard Seeds** (page 50), **Turmeric** (page 76)

Serves 4

Takes: 50 mins
Effort level: Easy

- 130 g (4½ oz/⅔ cup) basmati rice
- 200 g (7 oz/generous ¾ cup) red lentils
- 3 tablespoons olive oil
- 1 onion, finely sliced
- 5 cm (2 in) piece of fresh ginger root, finely grated
- 2 garlic cloves, crushed
- 2 teaspoons ground turmeric
- 2 teaspoons ground coriander
- 2 teaspoons cumin seeds
- 1–2 teaspoons medium chilli powder
- 1.2 litres (40 fl oz/4¾ cups) vegetable stock
- 200 g (7 oz) spinach
- 1 teaspoon black mustard seeds
- sea salt
- warm chapatis, to serve (optional)

Khichdi **or** ***khichri*** **is a South Asian dish made from rice and lentils. It's not dissimilar to a savoury porridge like the Chinese dish** ***congee*****, but while congee is often served quite plainly, khichdi is richly spiced. It's a go-to if you're under the weather, and in India it's often one of the first solid foods babies are fed. It's deeply comforting and very easy to make. There are lots of versions of khichdi around from many wonderful writers; this is just one.**

1. Tip the rice and lentils into a large sieve (fine mesh strainer) and rinse thoroughly under cold running water for 5 minutes to remove the starch. Set aside.

2. Heat 1 tablespoon of the oil in a large saucepan or casserole dish (Dutch oven) over a medium-high heat. Add the onion and a pinch of salt and fry for 10 minutes, or until golden. Stir through the ginger, garlic, turmeric, coriander, half the cumin seeds and the chilli powder and fry for a further 1 minute. Add the rice and lentils, then pour in the stock and bring to a simmer. Cover with a lid, reduce the heat to low and cook for 25 minutes, stirring occasionally, until the lentils have turned creamy and the rice is soft. Add the spinach and cook for a further 5 minutes, or until the spinach has wilted. If you prefer a thinner texture, add a splash of water to reach your preferred consistency.

3. To make a tadka (optional), heat the remaining oil in a small frying pan (skillet) over a medium heat. Add the rest of the cumin seeds and the black mustard seeds and cook for 1 minute. Spoon the lentils into 4 bowls, drizzle over the tadka and serve with warm chapatis, if you like.

Quick tips

- Cumin seeds are often seen in a mature Gouda in the Netherlands, as hard, mature cheeses team very well with cumin's slightly sweet, nutty flavour. Try sprinkling some on cheese on toast with a blob of mango chutney, or baking cumin seeds into a batch of cheese scones.
- You can make a tadka with ghee or butter instead of oil. Try adding curry leaves and alternative spices. Drizzle over dhal, curries or roasted vegetables (see Crispy Curry Leaf Roast Potatoes, page 175).

Spicy Chilli Oil and Cumin Lamb Noodles

Cumin (page 40), **Szechuan Peppercorns** (page 74)

Serves 4

Takes: 25 mins
Effort level: Easy

- 1½ tablespoons cumin seeds
- ½ teaspoon Szechuan peppercorns, crushed
- ½ tablespoon toasted sesame oil
- 400 g (14 oz) minced (ground) lamb
- 5 cm (2 in) piece of fresh ginger root, peeled and grated
- 1 fat garlic clove, crushed
- 6 spring onions (scallions), sliced
- 1 Chinese leaf cabbage, thickly shredded
- 4 tablespoons good-quality crispy chilli oil
- 1 tablespoon Chinese black vinegar
- 1 tablespoon dark soy sauce
- 350 g (12 oz) cooked noodles of your choice, such as egg, rice, udon, soba or belt noodles
- sesame seeds and Szechuan Pepper Smacked Cucumbers (page 170), to serve

A favourite restaurant for many in North London is X'ian Impressions, whose chefs are famous for their Shaanxi street food, and especially for their bowls of slurpy, hand-pulled belt noodles with cumin lamb. This recipe is inspired by that very dish, but uses a few cheats, like minced (ground) lamb, shop-bought noodles and a jar of good-quality chilli oil. These noodles are on the punchier side, with a hit of numbing heat from the ground Szechuan peppercorns, so tone down the chilli oil if you like things milder.

1. Toast the cumin seeds and Szechuan peppercorns in a dry frying pan (skillet) over a medium heat for 2 minutes. Transfer them to a spice grinder or pestle and mortar and grind to a coarse powder.

2. Heat the sesame oil in a wok or large frying pan over a high heat. Add the lamb and fry for 5–7 minutes, stirring frequently, until deep golden brown. Using a slotted spoon, transfer the lamb to a bowl and set aside.

3. Add the ground toasted spices to the pan, along with the ginger, garlic, most of the spring onions and the cabbage, and cook for 3 minutes. Stir in the chilli oil, vinegar, soy sauce and reserved lamb, then toss through the cooked noodles.

4. Serve the noodles in bowls, topped with the remaining spring onions and sesame seeds, with a bowl of smacked cucumbers on the side.

Extra ideas

- Crush Szechuan peppercorns and add them to salt to use as a seasoning on fried aubergines (eggplants), rice and noodles.
- Make a sticky marinade for firm tofu, chicken or pork ribs using 1 tablespoon crushed Szechuan peppercorns, 50 ml (1¾ fl oz/ 3 tablespoons) runny honey, 1 tablespoon rice wine vinegar and 3 tablespoons dark soy sauce.

Slow-cooked Chickpeas with Crispy House Blend Halloumi

House Blend (page 81)

Serves 4

Takes: 1 hr 30 mins
Effort level: Easy

- 2 tablespoons olive oil
- 2 onions, halved and sliced
- 1 large red (bell) pepper, seeded and sliced
- 1 garlic clove, crushed
- 1 tablespoon House Blend (page 81 to make your own), plus extra to serve
- 400 g (14 oz) tin chopped tomatoes
- 2 × 400 g (14 oz) tins chickpeas (garbanzos), drained but not rinsed
- 2–3 tablespoons rose harissa
- 1 teaspoon caster (superfine) sugar
- 1 teaspoon red wine vinegar
- 1 tablespoon tomato purée (paste)
- sea salt

For the halloumi
- 1 tablespoon cornflour (cornstarch)
- 2 teaspoons House Blend
- 220g (7¾ oz) halloumi, cubed
- 1 tablespoon olive oil

To serve
- Greek yoghurt
- small handful of parsley leaves
- flatbreads

The House Blend (page 81) we have used throughout this book is a mixture of Aleppo chilli pepper for hot-fruity notes, Urfa chilli pepper to bring a smokiness to the party, and cured sumac for a tangy, lemony finish. It's inspired by the Turkish tradition of using an everyday table spice to liberally sprinkle over dishes. It's often used as a finishing flavour – a little like salt or pepper – and makes pretty much everything taste better. Here, it's used to coat the crispy halloumi, as well as to finish the dish with a final flourish.

1. Heat the olive oil in a casserole dish (Dutch oven) over a medium heat. Add the onions and cook for 15 minutes, or until sticky and caramelised. Add the pepper and cook for 5 minutes, then stir through the garlic and House Blend and cook for a further 2 minutes. Add the tomatoes, chickpeas, harissa, sugar, vinegar and tomato purée and season with salt to taste. Cover with a tight-fitting lid, reduce the heat to low and cook for 1 hour, stirring occasionally.

2. When the chickpeas have about 10–15 minutes of cooking time left, prepare the halloumi. Line a small plate with baking parchment and set aside. Spread the cornflour and house blend over a medium plate, then toss the halloumi in the mixture until lightly coated all over. Heat the olive oil in a non-stick frying pan (skillet) over a medium heat and fry the halloumi for 10 minutes, or until evenly golden and crisp on all sides. Remove with a slotted spoon and transfer to the lined plate.

3. Serve the chickpeas with the crispy halloumi, torn parsley, a dollop of thick Greek yoghurt, an extra pinch of House Blend and lots of flatbreads for scooping.

Extra ideas

- Sprinkle House Blend on to poached or fried eggs or avocado toast to take brunch to the next level. You can also use it in marinades and dressings for an instant savoury hit.
- **House Blend garlic bread** – mash 1 tablespoon House Blend into 70g (2½ oz) softened unsalted butter, along with 1 small garlic clove, crushed, ½ small bunch chopped parsley and a pinch of sea salt. Halve a baguette lengthways and slather the butter over the cut sides. Grill under a hot grill on a baking tray for around 3 minutes or until lightly golden brown. Slice and serve.
- Toss a pinch of House Blend into cooked spaghetti with extra virgin olive oil and garlic for a spiced version of aglio e olio.

Kimchi and Togarashi Fried Rice

Shichimi Togarashi (page 66)

Serves 2

Takes: 25 mins
Effort level: Easy

- 3 tablespoons toasted sesame oil
- 5 cm (2 in) piece of fresh ginger root, peeled and grated
- bunch of spring onions (scallions), roughly chopped
- 2 pak choi, roughly chopped
- 250 g (9 oz/1⅓ cups) cooked Japanese short-grain rice or any other cooked rice
- 100 g (3½ oz) good-quality kimchi
- ½–1 teaspoon shichimi togarashi, plus extra to serve
- 1 tablespoon black or white sesame seeds
- 2 teaspoons rice vinegar
- 1 tablespoon dark soy sauce
- 2 eggs
- ½ small bunch of coriander (cilantro), torn
- sea salt
- crispy chilli oil, to serve (optional)

This quick fried rice is packed with the gut-loving Korean ferment kimchi. The shichimi togarashi gives it an extra hit of spice, and it's stir-fried with pak choi before being topped with a golden fried egg. You can have it on the table in less than 30 minutes, making it ideal for a busy weeknight. Add flaked fish, leftover roast chicken or fried firm tofu if you want to bulk it out.

1. Heat 2 tablespoons of the sesame oil in a large frying pan (skillet) over a medium heat. Add the ginger, spring onions and a pinch of salt and fry for 3 minutes, or until beginning to turn golden brown and caramelised. Add the pak choi and stir-fry for 5 minutes, or until softening. Increase the heat to medium-high, then add the rice and fry for a further 5 minutes. Stir through the kimchi, togarashi, sesame seeds, rice vinegar and soy sauce, and warm through for 2–3 minutes.

2. In a separate medium frying pan, heat the remaining sesame oil over a high heat for 1 minute. Crack the eggs into the pan and fry, undisturbed, for 2 minutes. Carefully swirl the oil around the pan to cook the whites for a further 1 minute.

3. Spoon the fried rice into 2 bowls, then top with the eggs, coriander, some extra togarashi and a splash of chilli oil, if you like it spicy.

Extra ideas

- Shichimi togarashi works really well with cream cheese. Try spreading a thick layer of cream cheese on to toasted sourdough or bagels with togarashi and a slick of hot chilli sauce.
- **Simple fish dinner** – Preheat the oven to 200°C fan (400°F/gas 7). Sprinkle shichimi togarashi over a salmon or cod fillet with 1 tablespoon unsalted butter and ½ tablespoon miso paste. Wrap in baking parchment and bake for 20 minutes for a speedy supper.

Roasted Carrots with Cold Green Yoghurt and Crispy Shallots

Nigella (page 51), **Garam Masala** (page 44), **Chilli** (page 32)

Serves 4

Takes: 25 mins
Effort level: Easy

- 300 g (10½ oz) carrots, tops trimmed and halved lengthways
- 1 tablespoon olive or rapeseed (canola) oil, plus extra for frying
- 1 teaspoon nigella seeds
- 1 teaspoon garam masala
- ½ teaspoon Kashmiri chilli powder
- 2 banana shallots, thinly sliced
- sea salt

For the green yoghurt
- ½ bunch of coriander (cilantro)
- ½ bunch of mint, plus extra leaves to serve (optional)
- 1 small garlic clove
- 300 g (10½ oz) full-fat (whole) Greek yoghurt
- ½ teaspoon sea salt

Sweet carrots sit well with nigella seeds and their slightly bitter, onion-like flavour. Here, they are combined with heady garam masala and Kashmiri chilli to create a showstopper of a dish you'll make time and time again: it turns a quid's worth of carrots into something truly spectacular. This can be served as a side dish as part of a wider meal, but it sits well on its own, too, so serve it for lunch with plenty of paratha or roti for dunking.

1. Preheat the oven to 180°C fan (350°F/gas 6). Toss the carrots in a large roasting tin (pan) with the 1 tablespoon oil, along with the nigella seeds, garam masala, chilli powder and some salt. Roast for 15 minutes.

2. Meanwhile, prepare the green yoghurt. Blitz the coriander, mint, garlic and half of the yoghurt to a fine paste in a food processor. Tip the remaining yoghurt into a large bowl, then fold in the blitzed mixture, along with the salt. Cover and chill in the refrigerator until needed. (It can be made up to 2 days ahead.)

3. Heat 2 cm (¾ in) oil for frying in a small frying pan (skillet) over a medium heat until bubbles start to float to the surface. To test if the oil is ready, add a small piece of shallot; it should turn golden and crispy in 30 seconds. Once the oil is ready, add the remaining shallots and fry for 1 minute, or until deep golden brown. Drain on paper towels and sprinkle with salt.

4. Spoon and swirl the yoghurt on to a serving plate. Top with the carrots and crispy shallots, and a few extra mint leaves, if you like, and serve.

Quick tips

- The pairing of nigella seeds and carrots can be extended into soups (see Carrot, Turmeric and Tamarind Soup, page 126).
- Nigella seeds are lovely melted into butter, then spooned on to roasted sweet potatoes or fried halloumi.

Easy Creamy Roasted Red Pepper and Urfa Pasta

Pul Biber (page 60)

Serves 4

Takes: 40 mins
Effort level: Easy

- 2 tablespoons olive oil
- 1 onion, finely chopped
- 1 fat garlic clove, chopped
- 2 teaspoons Urfa chilli (hot pepper) flakes or ½ teaspoon ordinary chilli flakes
- 400 g (14 oz) dried pasta, such as rigatoni or penne
- 450 g (1 lb) jar roasted red peppers, drained
- 130 g (4½ oz/½ cup) mascarpone
- 1 teaspoon white wine vinegar
- 40 g (1½ oz) Parmesan or vegetarian hard cheese, grated, plus extra to serve
- sea salt

This creamy, indulgent pasta recipe is a great one to have up your sleeve for long, dark, cold days. It's utter comfort in a bowl, and is quick to make, using a jar of roasted peppers, mascarpone and a pinch of chilli, gives the rich sauce a nice balanced kick at the end. Urfa is lovely because of its smokiness, but this would work well with any chilli you have on your spice rack. Rigatoni is my pasta of choice on this one; it's good for catching the sauce and extremely satisfying to eat.

1. Heat the olive oil in a large shallow casserole dish (Dutch oven) or frying pan (skillet) over a low- medium heat. Add the onion and a pinch of salt and fry for 10 minutes, or until softened and translucent. Add the garlic and chilli flakes and fry for 1 minute. Remove from the heat and leave to cool.

2. Bring a large saucepan of salted water to the boil. Add the pasta and cook until al dente. Drain, reserving 100–150 ml (3½–5 fl oz/scant ½–⅔ cup) of the cooking water.

3. Tip the peppers, cooled onion mixture, mascarpone and vinegar into a food processor and blitz until super smooth.

4. Tip the pepper sauce into a large frying pan with the pasta, Parmesan and 100 ml (3½ fl oz/scant ½ cup) of the reserved cooking water, adding more if the sauce needs loosening further. Bring to a bubble over a medium heat for 1–2 minutes and toss everything together. Season to taste with salt, then remove from the heat and divide between serving bowls. Top with extra Parmesan to serve. The sauce will keep in the refrigerator for up to a week or frozen for 3 months.

Extra ideas

- You can roast your own peppers for this dish. Simply, preheat the grill (broiler) to high, then grill (broil) 3 large red (bell) peppers for 20 minutes, or until blackened all over, then leave to cool before peeling off the charred skin, removing the seeds and slicing the flesh.
- Urfa pairs really well with all things red (bell) pepper – try adding it to a romesco sauce.

Blackened Sumac Salmon Grain Bowls with Tahini Dressing

Cumin (page 40), **Sumac** (page 70), **Paprika** (page 66)

Serves 2

Takes: 40 mins
Effort level: Easy

- 130 g (4½ oz) mixed quinoa
- 1½ tablespoons olive oil, plus extra for drizzling
- 3 tablespoons tahini
- juice of 2 large lemons
- 3–4 tablespoons water
- ½ red onion, very thinly sliced
- ½ cucumber, sliced
- 1 teaspoon + a pinch of sumac
- ½ teaspoon hot smoked paprika
- ½ teaspoon cumin
- 2 × 150 g (5 oz) salmon fillets
- 20 g (¾ oz) unsalted butter
- 2 eggs, soft-boiled for 6½ minutes (optional)
- 1 small, ripe avocado, sliced
- 1 tablespoon black or white sesame seeds
- cress or herbs of your choice, for sprinkling
- sea salt

This method uses the Caribbean cooking style of 'blackening'. The spice rub on the outside of the salmon is cooked over a high heat, giving it a deliciously smoky and crisp exterior with perfectly cooked fish in the centre. You can add your cooked fish to this grain bowl, but if you prefer, you can stuff it into pitta breads with tahini and parsley, or simply eat it with salad and potatoes.

What is blackening? It might feel counterintuitive to take the cooking quite so far, but don't lose your bottle, and overcome any concerns about burning your food – the key is a high heat on the outside. The method is called blackening because the point is to appropriately burn (blacken) the spice coating. The just-burnt spices against the oily fish give it an earthy, warm-flavoured coating rather than being super 'spicy' or bitter as you would expect.

1. Cook the quinoa according to the packet instructions. Drain in a sieve, then tip into a bowl and toss with a drizzle of olive oil and some salt. Set aside.

2. Mix together the tahini, the juice of 1 lemon, the water and a pinch of salt in a small bowl and set aside. In a separate medium bowl, combine the onion, cucumber, a pinch of the sumac, a pinch of salt and the remaining lemon juice and toss until combined. Leave to stand for 20 minutes.

3. Mix the olive oil, remaining sumac, paprika, cumin and a pinch of salt together in a small bowl. Use a pastry brush to brush the mix all over the salmon fillets.

4. Heat a heavy-based frying pan (skillet) over a high heat until almost smoking. Add the butter and a drizzle of olive oil, then flip the salmon, skin-side down, into the pan and cook for 3 minutes. Turn over and cook for a further 3–4 minutes until the skin and flesh are dark and crispy.

5. Spoon the quinoa into 2 serving bowls. Drizzle over the tahini dressing, then flake over the fish. Add a soft-boiled egg to each bowl, along with the avocado slices, cucumber salad, sesame seeds and cress or herbs. Serve.

Extra ideas

- For a simple, summery barbecue side dish, add a good pinch of sumac to a salad of tomatoes, olive oil, lemon juice and thinly sliced red onion.
- Sprinkle sumac over feta, cauliflower or potatoes before roasting for a punch of flavour.
- Mix flaky sea salt with sumac, store in a jar and use it as a zingy seasoning.
- **Sumac roast chicken** – Preheat the oven to 170°C fan (340°F/gas 5). Rub a whole 1.2 kg (2 lb 12 oz) chicken in a mixture of 50 g (2 oz) unsalted butter and 3 teaspoons sumac. Stuff thinly sliced preserved lemon under the skin and sprinkle with sea salt before roasting for 1 hour 15 minutes, or until the chickens juices run clear when a skewer is inserted into the thickest part.

Carrot, Turmeric and Tamarind Soup

Ginger (page 48), **Turmeric** (page 78), **Chilli** (page 32), **Cumin** (page 40), **Coriander** (page 36)

Serves 4–5

Takes: 50 mins
Effort level: Easy

- 3 tablespoons olive oil
- 1 onion, roughly chopped
- 2 fat garlic cloves, crushed
- 5 cm (2 in) piece of fresh ginger root, peeled and grated
- 2 teaspoons ground turmeric
- 2 teaspoons ground cumin
- 2 teaspoons ground coriander
- ½ teaspoon chilli (hot pepper) flakes
- 1 kg (2 lb 4 oz) carrots, chopped
- 1 litre (34 fl oz/4 cups) hot vegetable stock
- 400 ml (13 fl oz/generous 1½ cups) coconut milk
- 2 teaspoons tamarind paste
- sea salt
- plain or Greek yoghurt, to serve

For the chutney (optional)
- small bunch of coriander (cilantro)
- ½ small bunch of mint
- juice of ½ lemon
- 1 small garlic clove, roughly chopped
- 3 tablespoons olive oil

Carrots and their fellow roots ginger classically pair well with turmeric, and adding a few other storecupboard spices makes this vegan soup feel delicate and warming even though it's super simple. It has the added advantage of using tamarind – an ingredient which recipes often only call for a tiny measure of, and then it sits on your shelf looking lonely for the next six months. Adding it to vegetable soups is a great way to inject that acidic element and use up an ingredient that can be tricky to know what to do with.

1. Heat the olive oil in a large casserole dish (Dutch oven) over a low-medium heat. Add the onion and a pinch of salt and gently fry for 10 minutes until softened and translucent. Add the garlic, ginger, turmeric, cumin, coriander and chilli flakes and fry for 1 minute. Add the carrots, hot stock and coconut milk. Bring to a simmer, then cover with a lid and cook for 30 minutes, or until the vegetables are soft enough to cut through with a spoon. Add the tamarind and blend with a hand-held blender until smooth. Season to taste with plenty of salt.

2. To make the chutney, blitz together the coriander, mint, lemon juice, garlic, olive oil and some salt in a food processor to create a coarse chutney.

3. Ladle the soup into bowls, and serve topped with the chutney and a generous dollop of yoghurt. This soup will keep frozen for up to 6 months.

Extra ideas

- **Turmeric, fennel and ginger tea** – Put ½ teaspoon ground turmeric into a teapot with ½ teaspoon crushed fennel seeds, 5 cm (2 in) piece of peeled and sliced fresh ginger root and 1 lemon or small orange, thinly sliced. Pour in 600 ml (20 fl oz/2½ cups) boiling water. Steep for 5 minutes before straining into 2 mugs. Sweeten with honey.

Tomato, Za'atar and Butter Pasta

Za'atar (page 78)

Serves 2

Takes: 30 mins
Effort level: Easy

- 30 ml (1 fl oz/2 tablespoons) extra virgin olive oil
- 2 large garlic cloves, left whole
- 250 g (9 oz) cherry or piccolo tomatoes
- 1½ teaspoons za'atar
- 200 g (7 oz) bucatini, linguine or spaghetti
- 30 g (1 oz) Parmesan or vegetarian hard cheese, grated, plus extra to serve
- 15 g (½ oz) unsalted butter
- sea salt and freshly ground black pepper

There could not be an easier weeknight pasta. This classic Italian method of cooking fresh tomatoes in a layer of olive oil until they are popping and juicy gives you a quick and unctuous sauce. Adding za'atar gives it a lemony kick and herbiness, which is a fantastic addition. You could use this same method to cook tomatoes and serve them with cheesy polenta (cornmeal) or piled on to toast for another quick dinner idea.

1. Heat the olive oil in a large frying pan (skillet) over a medium heat. Add the garlic and leave to sizzle for 5 minutes, then turn off the heat and leave to stand for 10 minutes.

2. Scoop out the garlic and discard. Add the tomatoes to the garlic-infused oil and cook over a medium heat for 10 minutes until popping and juicy, with some still holding their shape. Add the za'atar and cook for 30 seconds.

3. Meanwhile, bring a large saucepan of well-salted water to the boil. Cook the pasta according to the packet instructions. Once cooked, remove the pasta with tongs and transfer to the tomato pan, along with the Parmesan and butter. Toss everything together over a medium heat for a few minutes. Season with salt, then serve in shallow bowls with extra Parmesan.

Extra ideas

- Za'atar is good with fatty cheese, so try it as a replacement for the pepper in Cacio a Pepe on page 111 or sprinkle it on top of macaroni cheese before baking.
- **Easiest za'atar pasta** – Mash together 50 g (2 oz) unsalted butter with 1 tablespoon za'atar, then toss this through hot pasta with lots of salt

Roasting Tin Chicken with Aleppo and Lemony Butter Beans

Pul Biber (page 60)

Serves 2

Takes: 55–60 mins
Effort level: Easy

- 3 tablespoons olive oil
- 4 large chicken legs
- 30 g (1 oz) unsalted butter
- 2 onions, thinly sliced
- 2 garlic cloves, thinly sliced
- 3 teaspoons Aleppo chilli pepper
- 2 × 400 g (14 oz) tins butter (lima) beans, drained
- 250 g (9 oz) small tomatoes (cherry or piccolo work well)
- 150 ml (5 fl oz/⅔ cup) chicken stock
- 1 lemon, half finely zested and half thinly sliced
- sea salt and freshly ground black pepper
- crusty bread, to serve (optional)

Everyone needs an everyday chicken recipe, one that requires little washing-up or hands-on time. You can make several different versions of this; try swapping the chicken legs for thighs, the butter (lima) beans for cannellini or chickpeas (garbanzos) and the chilli for any number of spices, from ras el hanout to hot smoked paprika. The chicken cooks in the buttery onion and tomatoes, which makes a glossy sauce good enough to mop off the plate with a hunk of bread.

1. Preheat the oven to 180°C fan (350°F/gas 6). Heat 1 tablespoon of the oil in a large non-stick frying pan (skillet) over a high heat. Season the chicken skin and fry, skin-side down, for 5 minutes, or until deep golden brown and crispy. Set aside in a roomy roasting tin (pan), skin-side up.

2. Heat the remaining oil with the butter in the same pan over a medium heat. When foaming, add the onions and fry for 15 minutes until soft and sticky. Add the garlic and 2 teaspoons of the Aleppo chilli pepper and cook for 1 minute. Stir through the butter beans, tomatoes, stock and lemon zest and season to taste. Spoon the beans and tomatoes around the chicken in the roasting tin. Nestle the lemon slices into the beans, then scatter the last of the chilli flakes over the chicken skin and roast for 30–35 minutes until cooked through.

3. Serve with crusty bread, if you like.

Extra ideas

- Sprinkle Aleppo chilli pepper on to hummus or baba ghanoush.
- Add Aleppo chilli pepper to marinades for barbecued meats, such as spatchcock chicken.
- Whisk some lemon juice, oil, Aleppo chilli pepper and finely grated garlic together in a bowl, then toss through some drained butter (lima) beans for an easy bean side salad.

Roasting Tin Aloo Chaat

Amchur (page 26), **Chilli** (page 32), **Cumin** (page 40),
Ginger (page 48), **Peppercorns** (page 58)

Serves 4

Takes: 1 hr
Effort level: Easy

- 4 medium potatoes (1 kg/2 lb 4 oz), peeled and cut into 4 cm (1½ in) chunks
- 3 tablespoons rapeseed (canola) or vegetable oil
- 1 teaspoon Kashmiri chilli powder or mild chilli powder
- 2 teaspoons chaat masala
- 1 teaspoon amchur powder
- ¼ teaspoon freshly ground black peppercorns
- 1 teaspoon ground cumin
- ½ onion, finely chopped
- 1 garlic clove, finely chopped
- 5 cm (2 in) piece of fresh ginger root, peeled and grated
- 4–5 tablespoons shop-bought tamarind sauce
- 50 g (2 oz) pomegranate seeds
- 50 g (2 oz) thin sev (savoury Indian snack)
- sea salt flakes
- chapati or naan, to serve

For the chutney

- juice of ½ lemon
- small bunch of mint
- small bunch of coriander (cilantro)
- 1 green chilli, sliced
- 20 g (¾ oz/⅛ cup) cashews or peanuts
- 1 teaspoon cumin seeds
- 7 tablespoons water
- pinch of sea salt

Aloo chaat is a vegetarian spiced potato dish that originated in northern India. It's the kind of dish that perfectly shows off how spices can be absorbed beautifully by the humble potato. Traditionally fried, this version roasts everything for weeknight ease, and is topped with crunchy and saucy sweet-and-sour toppings for a moreish mouthful. If you don't have time to make the coriander chutney, simply omit it for lots of coriander (cilantro) and sliced green chilli.

1. Tip the potatoes into a large saucepan, then cover with cold water and plenty of salt. Bring to the boil, then reduce the heat and simmer for 7 minutes. Drain and leave to steam-dry for 5 minutes, then tip out on to a large baking sheet and leave to dry for another 5 minutes.

2. Preheat the oven to 200°C fan (400°F/gas 7). Heat the oil in a shallow roasting tin in the oven for 10 minutes, then the potatoes and cook for 15 minutes. Remove from the oven and stir through the spices, onion, garlic and ginger, then return to the oven and cook for a further 20 minutes.

3. Meanwhile, for the chutney, blitz together all the ingredients in a food processor until smooth. Set aside.

4. Season the aloo chaat with lots of sea salt flakes. Drizzle over the chutney and tamarind sauce, and top with the pomegranate seeds and sev. Serve with chapati or naan on the side.

Extra ideas

- Use ground peppercorns liberally in rich curry sauces to add a hit of peppery spice.
- Add this combination of spices to homemade potato wedges and serve with mango chutney and yoghurt for dunking.

Weekend Feasts

Spiced Honey Scotch Bonnet Ham with Pineapple Rice

Allspice (page 24), **Cinnamon** (page 34), **Chilli** (page 32)

Serves 7–8

Takes: 3 hrs
Effort level: A little effort

- 2.5 kg (5 lb 10 oz) unsmoked or smoked boned and rolled gammon (ham) joint
- 1 onion, halved
- 1 carrot, roughly chopped
- 1 celery stalk, roughly chopped
- 1 fresh bay leaf
- 1 scotch bonnet chilli, halved
- ½ bunch of thyme, tied together with kitchen string
- coleslaw, to serve

For the glaze
- ½ teaspoon allspice
- 1 teaspoon dried thyme
- ½ teaspoon ground cinnamon
- ½ teaspoon ground cloves
- 100 g (3½ oz/scant ⅓ cup) clear runny honey
- ½ scotch bonnet chilli
- 50 g (2 oz) pineapple, peeled and cubed
- 1 tablespoon vegetable oil

Allspice takes centre stage in the rich and sticky glaze to this celebration ham. This is a good all-year-round dish, and is ideal for making on a Sunday as an alternative to a heavy roast in the warmer months. Inspired heavily by spices commonly used in dishes from the Caribbean, the sweet and spicy aromas of allspice, cloves, cinnamon and chilli work really well alongside the salty ham and baked rice. This ham will keep for up to 3 days in the refrigerator and is delicious cold in a sandwich or in a cheese and ham toastie with hot pepper sauce. It's also great chopped and stirred through any of the leftover rice.

1. Bring the ham to room temperature 2 hours before cooking: it will cook more evenly if it isn't chilled. Place the ham in a large, deep saucepan and add the onion, carrot, celery, bay leaf, chilli and thyme. Cover with cold water and place over a high heat. Bring to the boil, then reduce the heat to low–medium, cover with a lid and cook gently for 1 hour 40 minutes. Turn off the heat and leave the ham to stand in its cooking water for 30 minutes.

2. Line a large roasting tin (pan) with kitchen foil. Remove the ham from the pan and add to the prepared roasting tin, then leave to cool a little. Set the ham cooking water aside. You will need 650 ml (22 fl oz/2⅔ cups) of this liquid, so top it up with water if you don't have enough.

3. Preheat the oven to 200°C fan (400°F/gas 7). Using a sharp knife, remove the skin from the ham, then slash the thick layer of fat that's leftover in a criss-cross pattern.

4. For the glaze, blitz all the ingredients in a food processor until smooth. Brush half of this over the ham and roast for 15 minutes. Brush

continues overleaf

For the rice

- 80 g (3 oz) unsalted butter
- 1 onion, finely chopped
- 1 teaspoon garlic granules
- 1½ teaspoons allspice
- 2 teaspoons dried thyme
- 400 g (14 oz/2 cups) long-grain rice
- 300 g (10½ oz) pineapple, peeled and cubed
- 2 × 400 g (14 oz) tins kidney beans in water, drained
- 4 spring onions (scallions), finely sliced
- sea salt

the ham with the remaining glaze and roast for a further 10–15 minutes, or until golden and sticky. Leave to rest while you make the rice. Leave the oven on.

5. For the rice, heat the butter in a large ovenproof, lidded saucepan or casserole dish (Dutch oven) over a low-medium heat. Add the onion and a pinch of salt and fry gently for 15 minutes, or until softened and translucent. Add the garlic granules, allspice and dried thyme, and cook for 1 minute. Stir through the rice, pineapple and kidney beans, then pour over the reserved ham cooking water and bring to a simmer. Once the rice is simmering, cover with a lid and transfer to the oven for 20 minutes. Remove from the oven and leave to stand with the lid on for 10 minutes. Fluff up the rice, stir through the spring onions and season with salt.

6. Slice the ham and serve it alongside the pineapple rice and coleslaw.

Extra ideas

- Use allspice to make your favourite Jerk chicken recipe.
- Add a pinch of allspice to your favourite beef chilli, or try it in the Slow-cooked Ancho Beef Shin opposite.
- **Braised red cabbage wedges with allspice, cider and apples** – Melt 50 g (2 oz) unsalted butter in a casserole dish (Dutch oven) over a low heat and fry 2 thinly sliced red onions for 15 minutes, or until softened. Stir through ½ teaspoon allspice and 1 teaspoon ground cinnamon. Cut 1 red cabbage into 8 wedges. Nestle the wedges into the dish and pour over 150 ml (5 fl oz/⅔ cup) cider, 100 ml (3½ fl oz/scant ½ cup) cider vinegar, 400 ml (13 fl oz/generous 1½ cups) hot vegetables stock, 50 g (2 oz/¼ cup) soft brown sugar and 2 fresh bay leaves. Season with salt and bring to a simmer over a medium heat. Cook, uncovered, over a low-medium heat for 40–50 minutes until the cabbage is tender and the sauce glossy. Serve.

Slow-cooked Ancho Beef Shin

Coriander (page 36), **Cinnamon** (page 34), **Cumin** (page 40), **Chilli** (page 32), **Paprika** (page 56)

Serves 5

Takes: 2 hrs 30 mins
Effort level: A little effort

- 1 tablespoon olive oil
- 1 kg (2 lb 4 oz) beef shin, cut into 3 cm (1¼ in) pieces
- 1 onion, thinly sliced
- 1 garlic clove, crushed
- 2 teaspoons ancho chilli powder or medium chilli powder
- 2 teaspoons sweet smoked paprika
- 1 teaspoon ground coriander
- ½ teaspoon ground cinnamon
- 1 teaspoon cumin seeds
- 2 teaspoons dried oregano
- 2 tablespoons tomato purée (paste)
- 1 teaspoon caster (superfine) sugar
- 2 × 400 g (14 oz) tins chopped tomatoes
- 400 ml (13 fl oz/generous 1½ cups) hot beef stock, freshly boiled
- 400 g (14 oz) tin black beans or kidney beans, drained
- 1 tablespoon red wine vinegar
- 2 squares dark chocolate with at least 70% cocoa solids
- sea salt
- coriander (cilantro) leaves, to garnish

To serve
- freshly cooked rice
- avocado slices

Beef pairs so well with Mexican chillies, particularly ancho. Ancho is smoky with a mild-medium flavour and works well in slow-cooked dishes, standing up to bold flavours. Here, large chunks of beef shin are cooked in a base not dissimilar to that of chilli con carne until tender and buttery. Eat it in deep bowls with rice or in tortillas on cold nights.

1. Preheat the oven to 140°C fan (280°F/gas 3). Heat the olive oil in a lidded casserole dish (Dutch oven) over a high heat. Add the beef in batches and fry each batch for 5–7 minutes, turning the beef until it is deep golden brown. Set the meat aside on a plate.

2. Add the onion to the now-empty pan and cook for 5 minutes over a medium heat, then add the garlic, chilli powder, paprika, coriander, cinnamon, cumin seeds and oregano, and fry for 2 minutes. Return the beef to the pan, and add the tomato purée, sugar, chopped tomatoes and beef stock. Season to taste with salt. Transfer the pan to the oven and cook for 2 hours, or until the beef is tender. Thirty minutes before the end of cooking, add the beans, vinegar and chocolate. Leave to stand for 10 minutes before serving with rice and sliced avocado and garnishing with coriander.

Extra ideas

- Sprinkle thick wedges of watermelon with ancho chilli powder for a sweet and spicy snack, or swap the House Blend/pul biber for ancho in the Melon with House Blend, Feta and Mint (page 154).
- Add ancho chilli powder to a salsa or guacamole for a smoky, mild chilli twist.
- Mix honey with ancho chilli powder and drizzle it over a whole Camembert before baking until gooey.

Pepperonata, Coriander Seed, Charred Tomato and Burrata Salad

Chilli or Pul Biber (pages 32 or 60), **Coriander** (page 36)

Serves 4 as a starter (appetiser) and 2 as a lunch

Takes: 40 mins
Effort level: Easy

- 3 large red (bell) peppers
- 4 large ripe tomatoes, quartered
- 1 tablespoon coriander seeds
- pinch of chilli (hot pepper) flakes or Aleppo chilli pepper
- 1 tablespoon olive oil, plus extra for drizzling
- 1 tablespoon red wine vinegar
- 1 tablespoon capers, drained
- ½ teaspoon sea salt
- small handful of fresh basil leaves, torn
- 2 burrata cheeses
- toasted focaccia or sourdough, to serve

The combination of oozy burrata and crunchy, fragrant coriander seeds was made famous at Ottolenghi's London restaurant Nopi. He pairs his with sliced ripe peaches or blood orange according to the season. This salad, inspired by the fragrant pop of coriander seeds and its creamy cheese pairing, uses ripe summer tomatoes, (bell) peppers and a vinegar and caper dressing that cuts through the rich flavours. In the winter, swap the tomatoes and peppers for roasted long-stem broccoli or thickly sliced roasted Delicia pumpkin, for an equally delicious plateful.

1. Heat the grill (broiler) to its highest setting. Place the peppers under the grill and cook for 20–30 minutes, turning once, until blackened and charred. Set aside to cool completely, then peel off the skins, remove the seeds and slice the flesh into 1 cm (½ in) strips. Transfer to a bowl.

2. Heat a griddle pan over a high heat until almost at smoking point. Add the tomatoes and griddle for 1–2 minutes until they have char marks. Add these to the bowl with the peppers.

3. Add the coriander seeds and chilli flakes to a small, dry frying pan (skillet) and toast over a medium heat for 3 minutes until fragrant. Transfer to a pestle and mortar and lightly grind, then add to the bowl with the peppers and tomatoes. Whisk the olive oil and vinegar together in a small bowl, then pour this over the top. Stir in the capers, salt and most of the basil.

4. Spoon everything on to a plate and top with the burrata, the remaining basil and a drizzle of olive oil. Serve with toasted focaccia or sourdough.

Extra ideas

- Fry crushed coriander seeds in butter, then drizzle over a pumpkin soup.
- Use coriander seeds to top a dip – they work well on top of hummus or a yoghurt-based dip with lots of dill and olive oil.
- **Marinated spiced lemon olives** – Mix 150 g (5 oz/generous 1 cup) black and green olives (pitted or unpitted) with 150 ml (5 fl oz/⅔ cup) extra virgin olive oil, 1 sliced preserved lemon, 1 teaspoon crushed coriander seeds, 1 teaspoon fennel seeds and some sprigs of lemon thyme. Pour into a large jar, cover with a lid and leave to marinate in the refrigerator for 2 days. Enjoy alongside a cold drink as an aperitivo.

Slow-cooked Lamb with Prunes and Harissa

Cinnamon (page 34), **Coriander** (page 36), **Cumin** (page 40)

Serves 4

Takes: 3 hrs 30 mins
Effort level: Easy

- 2 tablespoons rapeseed (canola) or olive oil
- 1kg (1 lb 5 oz) lamb neck or shoulder, diced into 4 cm (1½ in) chunks
- 1 onion, sliced
- 1 carrot, roughly chopped
- 1 celery stalk, roughly chopped
- 2 fat garlic cloves, thinly sliced
- 1 teaspoon ground cinnamon
- 2 teaspoons coriander seeds, crushed
- 1 teaspoon ground cumin
- 500 ml (17 fl oz/2 cups) lamb stock
- 400 g (14 oz) tin chopped tomatoes
- 100 g (3½ oz/generous ⅓ cup) pitted prunes, roughly chopped
- 2 tablespoons rose harissa
- small handful of parsley, roughly chopped
- sea salt and freshly ground black pepper
- crispy potatoes, flatbreads or couscous, to serve

For the colder, winter evenings, it's great to have a one-pot in your repertoire. This dish is rich with slow-cooked lamb, prunes, cinnamon, coriander and cumin, and has a deep, warm flavour thanks to a couple of spoonfuls of rose harissa. It's an ideal freezer-filler to pull out when you're in need of comfort and substance.

1. Heat 1 tablespoon of the oil in a casserole dish (Dutch oven) over a high heat. Season the lamb with salt (not pepper, as this will burn), then add a third of the lamb to the pan and fry for 5–7 minutes, turning halfway through, until a deep, golden crust has formed. Set aside on a plate, then fry the remaining lamb in two more batches. Set the lamb aside.

2. Add the remaining oil to the now-empty pan, then add the onion, carrot and celery. Cook over a medium heat for 5 minutes, stirring occasionally. Add the garlic, cinnamon, coriander and cumin, and cook for 1 minute. Return the lamb to the pan, then add the stock, tomatoes, prunes and harissa and season to taste. Bring to the boil, then reduce the heat to low-medium, cover with a lid and cook for 1 hour 30 minutes–2 hours until the lamb is tender.

3. Check the seasoning, then finish with the parsley and serve with either crispy roast potatoes, flatbreads or couscous. This dish will keep chilled in the refrigerator for 3 days and frozen for 3 months. To reheat, defrost thoroughly and cook on the hob until the lamb is piping hot.

Quick tips

- Lamb and cinnamon are a beautiful flavour pairing – try adding a good pinch of ground cinnamon to lamb koftas or lamb meatballs.
- Sprinkle ground cinnamon and soft brown sugar on your porridge with a drizzle of single (light) cream.
- Add ground cinnamon to a coffee cake or chocolate recipe for a gentle spicing that brings out the rich coffee/cocoa flavours.

Crispy Pork Belly with Mojo Verde and White Beans

Coriander (page 36), **Fennel** (page 42), **Chilli** (page 32)

Serves 5–6

Takes: 3½ hrs, plus overnight chilling
Effort level: A little effort

- 1.3 kg (3 lb) boneless pork belly, skin on
- 1 tablespoon fennel seeds, crushed
- 2 tablespoons coriander seeds, crushed
- ½ teaspoon chilli (hot pepper) flakes
- 40 g (1½ oz/⅓ cup) sea salt flakes

For the fennel and beans
- 1 tablespoon olive oil
- 1 tablespoon unsalted butter
- 2 fennel bulbs, cut into wedges
- 100 ml (3½ fl oz/scant ½ cup) white wine
- 400 ml (13 fl oz/generous 1½ cups) chicken stock
- 3 × 400 g (14 oz) tins butter (lima) beans, drained

For the mojo verde
- 1 large garlic clove
- large bunch of coriander (cilantro) leaves
- 1 teaspoon ground coriander
- ½ teaspoon caster (superfine) sugar
- 100 ml (3½ fl oz/scant ½ cup) extra virgin olive oil
- 1 tablespoon red wine vinegar
- sea salt

Pork belly is a rich and fatty cut of meat that cries out for fragrant spices to cut through it. Rubbing the skin liberally with salt and a combination of fennel, coriander and chilli, then leaving it to marinate in the dry rub overnight, seasons and flavours the pork beautifully. Serve this with braised white beans and a punchy *mojo verde* sauce made from fresh coriander (cilantro), olive oil and vinegar. The sauce introduces an element of freshness and beautifully cuts through the rich flavours.

1. Score the pork skin with a sharp knife in 5 mm (¼ in) intervals. Lay the pork in a large roasting tin (pan).

2. Toast the fennel seeds, coriander seeds and chilli flakes in a dry frying pan (skillet) over a medium heat for 3–4 minutes. Add them to a mortar and crush them lightly with a pestle, then tip them into a bowl with the salt and mix together. Pack two-thirds of the salt mixture over the pork skin and leave to stand, uncovered, in the refrigerator overnight.

3. The next day, preheat the oven to 150°C fan (300°F/gas 3½). Remove the pork from the refrigerator and scrape off the salt mix. Pat well with paper towels to remove the moisture, then season with the remaining salt mix. Roast in the oven for 2 hours.

4. Meanwhile, for the fennel and beans, heat the olive oil and butter together in a large saucepan over a medium heat. Add the fennel and fry for 5 minutes. Pour in the wine, stock and beans and bring to a simmer.

5. After the pork has been cooking for 2 hours, reduce the oven temperature to 130°C fan (260°F/gas 2), then pour the beans and fennel around the pork and cook for a further 1 hour. Now, increase the oven temperature to its highest setting and lift the pork onto a baking tray (sheet) and cook for a final 10–15 minutes until the skin has crackled. Remove from the oven and cover with foil, then leave to rest for 30 minutes.

continues overleaf

6. For the mojo verde, blitz all the ingredients in a food processor until semi-smooth in texture. Season to taste with salt.

7. Carve the pork and serve with the fennel and beans and mojo verde.

Extra ideas

- Rub a 2kg shoulder of lamb with the same spice blend before slow-roasting tightly covered in foil, at 150°C fan (300°F/gas 3½) for 4-5 hours or until tender and falling apart.
- Toast coriander seeds and fennel seeds in a dry frying pan (skillet) and stored in a clean jar, then sprinkle over roasted (bell) peppers, use to marinate olives, or sprinkle on top of feta before baking.
- **Whole roast spiced cauliflower** – Preheat the oven to 200°C fan (400°F/gas 7). Mash 50 g (2 oz) unsalted butter with 1 teaspoon smoked paprika, 1 tablespoon crushed coriander seeds and 1 teaspoon crushed fennel seeds. Trim the base of the cauliflower so it sits neatly in a roasting tin (pan), making sure its leaves are still attached. Rub the cauliflower all over with the butter mixture, a good pinch of salt and glug of olive oil. Roast, uncovered, for 20–25 minutes, basting frequently with the buttery juices. Carve and serve as a side dish to a grain salad.

'Nduja and Fennel Seed Meatballs

Fennel (page 42)

Serves 4

Takes: 50 mins
Effort level: A little effort

- 400 g (14 oz) minced (ground) pork
- 50 g (2 oz) 'nduja sausage
- ½ tablespoon fennel seeds, crushed
- ½ small bunch of parsley, finely chopped
- 70 g (2½ oz/generous ¾ cup) fine fresh white breadcrumbs
- 1 medium egg
- 1 tablespoon olive oil, for frying
- 400 g (14 oz) spaghetti or tagliatelle
- 1 heaped teaspoon sea salt
- grated Parmesan, to serve
- small handful of basil leaves, to serve

For the sauce

- 3 tablespoons olive oil
- 1 onion, very finely chopped
- 1 fat garlic clove, crushed
- 3 × 400 g (14 oz) tins finely chopped tomatoes (see Note below)
- bunch of herbs, tied together (rosemary, bay, oregano)
- 2 teaspoons caster (superfine) sugar
- 50 ml (1¾ fl oz/3 tablespoons) full-fat (whole) milk
- sea salt

Note: If you can't find tins of finely chopped tomatoes, then blitz them in a food processor before using.

Fennel, with its warm, sweet edge, teams well with pork and especially well with pork and chilli. This is a combination often seen in Italy in the likes of a *porchetta*. The hot hit of chilli in this recipe comes from a generous scoop of the Calabrian spicy sausage 'nduja. 'Nduja has gained popularity in the last few years, being stirred through pasta, melted on to oozy cheese pizzas and spread on toast. It adds a deep richness and punch of flavour to meatballs. The perfect meatball should have a good ratio of soft breadcrumbs to minced (ground) pork, as this gives it the squidgier, comforting texture that we should all be looking for.

1. Add the pork, 'nduja, fennel seeds, parsley, breadcrumbs, egg and salt to a large bowl and squish everything together with your hands for around 5 minutes. Divide into 12 equal-size balls, weighing for accuracy as you go. Set aside on a large plate, cover and chill until needed (these can be kept chilled in the fridge for up to 48 hours or frozen for 3 months – defrost them before cooking).

2. To make the sauce, heat the olive oil in a casserole dish (Dutch oven) over a low heat. Add the onion and a pinch of salt and fry gently for 10 minutes, or until softened and translucent. Add the garlic and cook for 1 minute. Stir through the tomatoes, herbs, sugar and a good pinch of salt, and simmer, uncovered, over a low-medium heat for 10 minutes. Stir through the milk, then blitz all the ingredients together with a hand-held blender for a smooth sauce, or keep it chunkier if you prefer.

3. To cook the meatballs, heat the 1 tablespoon olive oil in a large non-stick frying pan over a medium heat. Add the meatballs and cook for 5–7 minutes, turning occasionally with tongs, until evenly golden brown. Add the meatballs to the sauce, cover with a lid and simmer over a medium heat for 15 minutes, or until cooked through.

continues overleaf

4. Cook the pasta in a large saucepan of salted water according to the packet instructions, reserving around 120 ml (4 fl oz/½ cup) of the starchy cooking water. Drain the pasta and toss with the sauce and meatballs, adding a splash of the pasta water to loosen. Divide between bowls and serve topped with grated Parmesan and a few basil leaves.

Extra ideas

- Pork pairs beautifully with the aniseed hit of fennel. Try adding fennel to a sausage stew or sausage meat-based stuffing, along with some dried apricots.
- Try tossing 1 tablespoon fennel seeds and the finely grated zest of 1 lemon into your roast potatoes halfway through cooking. This pairs well with roast chicken or fried fish.

Ancho Prawn, Fregola and Charred Corn Salad

Chilli (page 32), **Coriander** (page 36), **Paprika** (page 56)

Serves 4

Takes: 40 mins
Effort level: Easy

- 3 whole corn-on-the-cobs
- 200 g (7 oz/generous ¾ cup) fregola, giant couscous or pearl couscous
- 300 g (10½ oz) extra-large king prawns (jumbo shrimp)
- 1 tablespoon extra virgin olive oil
- 3 teaspoons ancho chilli powder
- 1 teaspoon ground coriander
- ½ teaspoon sweet smoked paprika
- large bunch of coriander (cilantro), half chopped, half torn
- 4 spring onions (scallions), thinly sliced
- sea salt

For the dressing

- 3 limes, grated zest of 1 and juice of all 3, plus extra wedges to serve
- 4 tablespoons rapeseed (canola) oil or olive oil
- ½ garlic clove, finely grated
- ½ red chilli, seeded and thinly sliced
- 1 green chilli, seeded and thinly sliced

Ancho, as one of the milder Mexican chillies, has a mellow fruitiness that lends itself well to pairing with other fragrant flavours, such as lime and coriander. The fregola (a small pasta shape from Sardinia) gives this salad a substantial bite that takes it into dinner or lunch territory. If you want to enjoy it as a side, simply omit the prawns (shrimp) and increase the amount of corn. It's delicious served alongside smoky barbecued meats.

1. Bring a large saucepan of water to the boil. Add the whole corn-on-the-cobs and boil for 5 minutes, then drain and leave to steam-dry for 5 minutes. Heat a large griddle or frying pan (skillet) over a high heat. Add the corn and cook for 15 minutes, turning frequently until blackened and charred. Set aside to cool.

2. Cook the fregola in a saucepan of salted water according to the packet instructions. Drain and leave to cool slightly before transferring to a large bowl. Sit the corncobs on their ends and, using a serrated knife, cut downwards to remove the corn kernels. Stir these into the fregola. Set aside.

3. To make the dressing, whisk together the lime zest and juice, rapeseed oil and garlic in a small bowl. Add the chillies and season with salt.

4. Shell the prawns if they are not shelled already. Heat the extra virgin olive oil in a non-stick frying pan over a high heat, then add the prawns and fry for 1 minute. When they begin to turn pink, quickly mix in the ancho chilli powder, ground coriander and paprika, and cook for a further 1 minute. Season with salt.

5. Pour the dressing over the fregola and corn, then add the chopped coriander and spring onions and toss together. Pile on to a serving plate, then top with the prawns and torn coriander and serve.

Quick tips

- Add 2 teaspoons ancho chilli powder to your favourite chilli con carne recipe.
- Sprinkle ancho chilli powder over fried eggs and serve on top of toasted tortillas with grated cheese, avocado and pico de gallo (salsa).

Spinach and Nutmeg Gnocchi

Nutmeg (page 52)

Serves 5–6

Takes: 1 hr 40 mins
Effort level: A weekend challenge

- rock salt, for the baking sheet
- 1.5 kg (3 lb 5 oz) potatoes, such as Maris Piper or Desiree
- 350 g (12 oz) baby spinach
- 3 medium egg yolks
- semolina, for dusting
- ¾ whole nutmeg, grated
- 200 g (7 oz/1⅔ cups) 00 flour, plus extra for dusting
- 2 teaspoons sea salt, plus extra to taste
- freshly ground black pepper

For the brown butter
- 200 g (7 oz) unsalted butter
- 30 sage leaves
- juice of 1 large lemon

Homemade gnocchi takes a few steps and a little effort to make, but you are left with perfectly light potato nuggets that can be tossed into a rich and lemony brown butter, or stirred into homemade tomato *sugo* (tomato butter sauce). These basic gnocchi are enriched with spinach and nutmeg, turning them a deep green colour and lending a slightly nutty flavour. Make a large batch and freeze them for times when you are in search of comfort or need to feed a group of hungry friends.

1. Preheat the oven to 200°C fan (400°F/gas 7).

2. Spread a generous layer of rock salt on to a large rimmed baking sheet and sit the potatoes on top. Roast for 50–60 minutes until tender when a cutlery knife is inserted. Leave to cool for 10 minutes, then peel off and discard the still-warm skins. Pass the potatoes through a potato ricer or push through a sieve (fine mesh strainer) with a spoon on to a clean work surface and leave to cool.

3. Tip the spinach into a large saucepan with 2 tablespoons water and steam over a medium heat for 3 minutes, or until the spinach has wilted. Drain and leave to cool, then tip the spinach into a clean J-cloth and squeeze out any excess liquid. Finely chop, then add to a food processor with the egg yolks and blitz until smooth.

4. Dust a large baking sheet with semolina and set aside. Add the spinach mixture to the potato, along with the grated nutmeg, pasta flour and salt, and gently knead everything together with your hands until you have a uniform dough – don't overwork it. Divide the dough into 4 portions. Lightly dust the work surface with pasta flour, then roll each portion out into a long sausage, about 2 cm (¾ in) in diameter. Cut each sausage into 1.5–2 cm (⅝–¼ in) nuggets. You can keep them like this or roll ridges on to to them with the back of a fork or a ridged pasta paddle. Set aside on the prepared baking sheet. (At this stage, the gnocchi can be frozen on the baking sheet, then transferred to freezerproof bags once frozen and stored in the freezer for up to 6 months. Cook straight from frozen in a large saucepan of well-salted boiling water until they bob to the surface of the pan.)

5. When you are ready to cook, bring a large saucepan of well-salted water to the boil. Add the gnocchi and cook for 2–3 minutes until they bob to the surface.

6. For the brown butter, melt the butter in a large frying pan (skillet) over a medium heat until foaming. Add the sage and cook for 3–4 minutes until the butter begins to turn golden brown and smells biscuity, and the sage curls and becomes crispy. Squeeze in the lemon juice, add a good pinch of salt and the drained gnocchi, and toss everything together until the gnocchi is glossy and well coated.

7. Spoon the gnocchi on to plates and finish with a little pepper.

Extra ideas

- Alternatively, serve with a tomato butter sugo – for the sugo, heat 3 tablespoons unsalted butter and 1 tablespoon olive oil together over a low-medium heat. Add 1 finely chopped onion and a pinch of salt, and fry for 10–12 minutes until softened. Add 1 large crushed garlic clove and a pinch of chilli (hot pepper) flakes and fry for 1 minute. Add 2 × 400 g (14 oz) tins chopped tomatoes, ½ tablespoon caster (superfine) sugar and a good pinch of salt, and bring to a simmer. Cook, uncovered, over a low heat for 15–20 minutes, stirring frequently. After this time, blitz with a hand-held blender or in a food processor until smooth.
- Liberally grate nutmeg on buttered toast or crumpets.
- Roast pumpkin wedges in olive oil, nutmeg and Aleppo chilli pepper for an easy spiced autumnal (fall) side dish.
- Finish a mushroom or cheese risotto with a good grating of nutmeg and some crispy fried sage.
- Make a dauphinoise with potatoes, squash or celeriac (celery root), and grate over ½ nutmeg before baking in the oven.

Melon with House Blend, Feta and Mint

House Blend or Pul Biber (pages 81 and 60)

Serves 4 as a main or 6 as a side

Takes: 15 mins,
plus 15 mins chilling
Effort level: Very easy

- 70 ml (2½ fl oz/generous 4½ tablespoons) extra virgin olive oil
- juice of 2 lemons
- 1 tablespoon House Blend (page 81) or Aleppo chilli pepper
- 1 teaspoon dried mint
- 1 teaspoon sea salt
- 500 g (1 lb 2 oz) honeydew or cantaloupe melon, cut into 5 cm (2 in) cubes
- 500 g (1 lb 2 oz) watermelon, cut into 5 cm (2 in)
- 200 g (7 oz) feta, cut into chunks
- ½ small bunch of mint, leaves torn

Melon is no stranger to a hit of dried chilli and salt. In South and Central American countries, the pairing is common – and for good reason. The sweet and refreshing bite of melon and the contrast of a punch of heat makes for a satisfying salad. In this case, House Blend is used, harnessing heat from the pul biber and a tanginess from the sumac. Feta and mint tie it all together for a moreish salad best eaten at the height of summer, when the melons are at their peak.

1. Whisk together the olive oil, lemon juice, House Blend or Aleppo pepper, dried mint and salt together in a bowl.

2. Combine the different types of melon in a large bowl. Pour over the dressing and toss to combine, then leave to stand in the refrigerator for 15 minutes. Add the feta and top with the torn mint to serve. This will keep in the refrigerator for up to 3 days.

Extra ideas

- Sprinkle ½ teaspoon of House Blend on avocado on toast to pep up a brunch.
- Melt 50 g butter with 1 teaspoon House Blend, then drizzle it on soups, use it to fry eggs or simply toss it with spaghetti for a speedy dinner.
- Stir 1–2 teaspoons House Blend through cooked grains or beans, then add olive oil and lemon juice for a quick lunch.
- Use House Blend in the Chilli and Honey Fried Halloumi on page 182.
- **Feta and House Blend dip** – Blitz together 150 g (5 oz/⅔ cup) Greek yoghurt, ½ small garlic clove, 150 g (5 oz) crumbled feta, the leaves of ½ small bunch of mint and ½ small bunch of dill in a food processor until smooth and creamy, then fold through an extra 100 g (3½ oz/scant ½ cup) Greek yoghurt, 1 teaspoon House Blend and some salt. Spoon into a serving bowl, drizzle with extra virgin olive oil and sprinkle over some extra House Blend. Serve with crackers, crisps (chips) or crudités.

Togarashi Fried Chicken

Shichimi Togarashi (page 66)

Serves 4

Takes: 50 mins, plus overnight chilling
Effort level: A weekend challenge

- 8 skinless, boneless chicken thighs
- 3 heaped teaspoons fine sea salt
- 500 ml (17 fl oz/2 cups) buttermilk
- 200 g (7 oz/generous 1 cup) rice flour
- 100 g (3½ oz/generous ¾ cup) cornflour (cornstarch)
- 3½ teaspoons baking powder
- 2 teaspoons garlic granules
- 2 tablespoons shichimi togarashi, plus extra for sprinkling
- ½ teaspoon freshly ground black pepper
- 1 litre (34 fl oz/4 cups) vegetable oil, for deep-frying

For the mayonnaise

- 130 g (4½oz/½ cup) mayonnaise
- 2 teaspoons hot chilli sauce
- grated zest and juice of ½ lime

The perfect, top-tier level fried chicken should have a deeply golden, extra-crispy exterior and melt-in-the-mouth succulent interior. Its batter should be lightly spiced and well seasoned. Renowned food writer and London-based caterer Milli Taylor makes the most astonishing fried chicken, marinated in a buttermilk soak, then dry-coated in a mix of rice flour, baking powder and cornflour (cornstarch) for a beautiful crunch. She has very kindly gifted this recipe to this book. The spices in her original recipe have been switched out to shichimi togarashi in order to introduce some heat, but you could use za'atar or House Blend (page 81) if you fancy mixing things up.

1. Cut each chicken thigh into quarters, then tip into a large bowl. Add 2 teaspoons of the salt, then pour over the buttermilk and mix well. Cover and leave to chill in the refrigerator overnight.

2. The next day, combine the rice flour, cornflour, baking powder, garlic granules, shichimi togarashi, the remaining 1 teaspoon salt and the pepper in a medium bowl. Drop the brined chicken pieces into the mixture, 4 at a time, and toss lightly to coat well. Gently shake off any excess, then arrange on a large baking sheet.

3. Heat the oil for deep-frying in a large, deep saucepan (ensuring it is no more than two-thirds full) to 170°C (325°F), or until a cube of bread dropped in browns in 30 seconds. Deep-fry the chicken in small batches for 3–4 minutes at a time until golden and cooked through. Working in batches will help keep the oil at the right temperature and ensure you don't overcrowd the pan.

4. Using tongs, remove the fried chicken pieces to a clean dish towel to drain any excess oil, then transfer to a wire rack to ensure they stay crisp. Alternatively, arrange the fried chicken on a clean baking sheet and keep warm and crisp in a low oven.

5. For the mayonnaise, mix together the mayonnaise, hot sauce and lime zest and juice in a small bowl. Arrange the chicken on a serving platter, sprinkle with extra shichimi togarashi, and serve with the mayonnaise. Enjoy any leftovers in a brioche bun with kimchi, slaw or shredded lettuce.

Crab and Togarashi Mac and Cheese

Shichimi Togarashi (page 66)

Serves 6

Takes: 1 hr
Effort level: A little effort

- 950 ml (32 fl oz/generous 3¾ cups) full-fat (whole) milk
- 50 g (2 oz) unsalted butter
- 50 g (2 oz/generous ⅓ cup) plain (all-purpose) flour
- 350 g (12 oz) cheese – a mix of Gruyère, Comté, Red Leicester, Cheddar, grated
- ½–1 tablespoon hot sauce, to taste (siracha works well)
- 350 g (12 oz) dried macaroni
- 200 g (7 oz) fresh white and brown crab meat
- ½–1 tablespoon shichimi togarashi
- sea salt and freshly ground black pepper

A mix of cheeses for your mac and cheese is essential. If you just use Cheddar it may split due to its high fat content leaving you with oily pockets and a grainy sauce, so try to use at least three cheeses. The addition of a hard cheese like Comté or Gruyère gives you a nutty flavour, and the Red Leicester is there for its mellowness and colour. Crab makes this dish extra indulgent, and its salty sea flavour is perfect with the rich, cheesy sauce. To cut through this richness is shichimi togarashi, with its punchy chilli and slightly citrussy aroma. This is a Friday-night kind of dinner; enjoy with a bottle of cold white wine or some chilled beers. Serve it with a green salad, if you like.

1. Preheat the oven to 180°C fan (350°F/gas 4).

2. Warm the milk in a small saucepan over a low heat until steaming, then remove from the hob. Heat the butter in a large saucepan over a medium heat until foaming, then stir through the flour to make a thick paste and fry for 1 minute. Remove the pan from the heat and whisk in the warmed milk in several additions until you have a thin, smooth consistency. Return to a medium heat and whisk constantly for 5 minutes, or until the sauce has thickened. Add 300 g (101/2 oz) of the cheese, along with the hot sauce to taste and a pinch of salt. Whisk again until smooth (the sauce will look very thin, but thickens significantly in the oven).

3. Cook the pasta in a large saucepan of well-salted boiling water for 3 minutes, then drain and tip it into the cheese sauce. Stir to combine, then pour everything into a large ovenproof dish. Top with the remaining cheese and push in spoonfuls of the crab. Sprinkle with the shichimi togarashi and bake for 15 minutes. Leave to stand for 10 minutes before serving.

Extra ideas

- **Togarashi cheese on toast** – Pile slices of toast with grated cheese and a generous sprinkle of shichimi togarashi before grilling (broiling).
- **Togarashi chips** – Make your own chips (fries) and top them with ½–1 tablespoon shichimi togarashi. Serve with lots of mayonnaise.
- **Togarashi crisps** – Toss a 150 g (5 oz) bag of salted potato crisps (chips) with ½ tablespoon shichimi togarashi for a quick way to pep up a nibble or snack.

Za'atar Fried Fish with Preserved Lemon Tartare

Za'atar (page 78)

Serves 4

Takes: 1 hr
Effort level: A little effort

- 600 g (1 lb 5 oz) sustainable skinless, boneless white fish fillets, such as hake, haddock or Dover sole
- 50 g (2 oz/scant ½ cup) plain (all-purpose) flour
- 2 eggs, beaten
- 100 g (3½ oz/1⅔ cups) dried panko breadcrumbs
- 2 tablespoons za'atar
- rapeseed (canola) or sunflower oil, for frying
- sea salt and freshly ground black pepper

For the tartare
- 150 g (5 oz/⅔ cup) mayonnaise
- juice of ½ lemon
- 1 preserved lemon, inside scooped out and skin finely chopped
- 1 tablespoon baby capers
- 3 cornichons, chopped
- ½ banana shallot, finely chopped
- small bunch of dill, finely chopped
- 1 teaspoon za'atar

To serve
- baby gem lettuce, shredded
- brioche buns, white bread or chips (fries)

With Za'atar's citrussy notes means that it works particularly well with fish. Eat the panko breadcrumb-coated fish alongside chips (fries) or piled into buns with tartare sauce. This dish has an element of nostalgia, and it's easier than you think to make a cracking homemade fish and chips. The addition of chopped preserved lemon to the tartare gives it an intensely lemony flavour, but you can swap this for finely grated lemon zest, if you like.

1. Cut the fish into 8 chunky fingers, each about 4 cm (1½ in) in width. Tip the flour, eggs and panko into 3 separate shallow bowls. Mix 1 tablespoon of the za'atar into the flour and th other into the breadcrumbs Dip each fish finger into the flour, followed by egg, then the breadcrumbs. Set aside on a rimmed baking sheet, cover and leave in the refrigerator until ready to cook (these will keep for up to 24 hours).

2. For the tartare, mix together the mayonnaise, lemon juice, preserved lemon, capers, cornichons, shallot and dill in a medium bowl. Season gently with a little salt and pepper.

3. Line a baking sheet with paper towels. Heat 3 cm (1¼ in) of the oil for frying in a large, non-stick frying pan (skillet) over a medium heat and fry each fish finger for 5 minutes, turning halfway, until crispy and a deep golden brown. Set aside on a plate and sprinkle with a little salt.

4. Serve the fish fingers with the tartare and lettuce, sandwiched between soft buns or with a pile of chips.

Extra ideas

- Sprinkle za'atar on literally any fish and it will be delicious. Try baking salmon or trout in parcels of baking parchment with za'atar and oil, or cooking prawns (shrimp) in za'atar butter.
- Add za'atar to the scampi or tempura batter.

Togarashi Prawn Cocktail

Shichimi Togarashi (page 66)

Serves 6

Takes: 15 mins
Effort level: Easy

- 130 g (4½ oz/½ cup) mayonnaise
- 100 g (3½ oz/½ cup) sour cream
- 3 tablespoons tomato ketchup
- a good shake of Tabasco sauce
- juice of ½ lemon, plus wedges to serve
- 1 large romaine lettuce, shredded
- 150 g (5 oz) cooked king prawns (shrimp)
- 170 g (6 oz) cold-water Atlantic prawns (jumbo shrimp)
- 1 teaspoon shichimi togarashi, plus extra to taste
- sea salt

The prawn cocktail is the ultimate retro salad. Made popular by British home cook Fanny Craddock in the 1960s, it is brought into the modern era with a pinch of Japanese shichimi togarashi. With its combination of chilli, sesame and orange peel, it pairs well with the prawns (shrimp) and lends the dish a delicious kick of heat. Serve it on a platter, spoon it into dainty cocktail glasses or pile it into a sandwich.

1. Mix together the mayonnaise, sour cream, ketchup, Tabasco and lemon juice in a large bowl. Season to taste with a little salt.

2. Spread out the lettuce on a sharing plate, then top with the prawns, followed by the sauce. Finish with the shichimi togarashi, adding more if you like it spicier, and serve with lemon wedges. This mixture can also be packed into soft sliced wholemeal bread or rolls for a prawn cocktail sandwich.

Extra ideas

- **Miso and shichimi togarashi cod** – Mix 1 tablespoon white or brown miso with ½ tablespoon shichimi togarashi and 50 g (2 oz) softened unsalted butter. Fry 2 × 150 g (5 oz) cod fillets for 8 minutes over a medium heat, then throw the butter into the pan and use it to baste the cod.
- Sprinkle shichimi togarashi on soft-boiled or fried eggs, avocado on toast or in a cheese toastie.
- Add 1 teaspoon shichimi togarashi to a packet of instant ramen noodles to pep them up!

Paneer Makhani Pie

Cumin (page 40), **Garam Masala** (page 44), **Turmeric** (page 76), **Chilli** (page 32), **Cinnamon** (page 34), **Nigella** (page 51)

Serves 5

Takes: 1 hr 45 mins, plus overnight marinating
Effort level: A little effort

- 500 g (1 lb 2 oz) paneer, cut into large chunks
- 1 tablespoon vegetable oil
- 250 g (8 oz) Greek yoghurt
- 2 teaspoons Kashmiri or mild chilli powder
- 2 teaspoons ground cumin
- 1 teaspoon garam masala
- 1 teaspoon ground turmeric
- 3 large garlic cloves, grated
- 1 teaspoon sea salt
- 320 g (11¼ oz) ready-rolled all-butter puff pastry
- plain (all-purpose) flour, for dusting
- 1 egg, beaten
- 2 teaspoons nigella seeds
- cooked basmati rice, to serve

For the sauce
- 1 tablespoon vegetable or rapeseed (canola) oil
- 50 g (2 oz) unsalted butter
- 1 onion, finely chopped
- 10 cardamom pods, bashed
- 1 cinnamon stick, bashed in half
- 1 green chilli, halved lengthways
- 1 teaspoon Kashmiri chilli powder
- 2 teaspoons garam masala
- 3 tablespoons tomato purée (paste)
- 200 g (7 oz) tinned chopped tomatoes, blitzed until smooth
- 1 tablespoon cashew nut butter
- 200 ml (7 fl oz/scant 1 cup) double (heavy) cream
- 130 ml (4½ fl oz/½ cup) water
- 2 teaspoons honey
- sea salt

Originating in India, paneer makhani is a dish with a creamy gravy, usually made with butter, cream, tomatoes and spices. Paneer is the most common cheese used in India. It has a firm texture and milky taste, making it good for soaking up flavoursome sauces. This recipe bakes the dish into a puff pastry pie for added comfort and indulgence; it's fantastic served alongside a basmati or pilau rice. It's a great dish for hosting friends, or when you want a vegetarian showstopper: pure comfort and indulgence, perfectly spiced and richly spiked with cream.

1. Tip the paneer into a large bowl with the oil, yoghurt, spices, garlic and salt and mix everything together with your hands until the paneer is well coated. Cover and leave to chill in the refrigerator for 3 hours, or overnight.

2. The next day, heat the grill (broiler) to its highest setting. Line a rimmed baking sheet with kitchen foil. Spread the paneer out on to the prepared baking sheet in a single layer (this can be done in 2 batches if your tray isn't large enough) and grill (broil) for 7–10 minutes, or until lightly charred, turning halfway through, until the paneer is charred and blackened in places.

3. For the sauce, heat the oil and butter in a large shallow casserole dish (Dutch oven) or frying pan (skillet) over a low heat. Add the onion, cardamom, cinnamon and chilli and fry for 12 minutes, or until the onion is softened and translucent. Add the Kashmiri chilli powder, garam masala and tomato purée and fry for 2 minutes. Add the chopped tomatoes, cashew butter, cream and water. Tip in the paneer and any juices that have collected at the bottom of the sheet and stir everything together. Increase the heat to low–medium and simmer gently for 10 minutes. Season with salt and stir through the honey. Take the pan off the heat and leave to cool for 30 minutes, then remove and discard as many of the whole spices as you can find.

continues overleaf

4. Spoon the filling into a 23 cm (9 in) deep lipped pie dish. Roll the pastry out on a lightly floured work surface until a little bigger than the pie dish (about 25 cm/10 in), then lay it over the filling. Trim the edges with a sharp knife, then crimp the sides with a fork. Brush with the beaten egg and sprinkle with the nigella seeds. Freeze for 15 minutes; this helps the pastry to rise evenly and stay flaky.

5. Meanwhile, preheat the oven to 180°C fan (350°F/gas 6). Bake the pie for 35–45 minutes until deep golden brown and puffed up. Leave to rest for 10 minutes before serving with cooked basmati rice.

Extra ideas

- Garam masala is an easy spice to add to a roasting tin (pan) of roasted vegetables for a medley of aromatic flavours – try it with roots, such as parsnips, carrots or celeriac (celery root), or with cauliflower or Brussels sprouts.
- Finish a bowl of homemade raita with a pinch of garam masala.
- Mash 1 tablespoon Kashmiri chilli powder with 100 g (3½ oz) salted butter, then melt it on barbecued prawns (shrimp) or corn-on-the-cob.

Roasted Cauliflower Wedge Coronation Salad

Garam Masala (page 44), **Turmeric** (page 76), **Chilli** (page 32), **Nigella** (page 51)

Serves 4

Takes: 45 mins
Effort level: Easy

- 50 g (2 oz/generous ½ cup) flaked (slivered) almonds
- 1 large cauliflower
- 3 teaspoons garam masala
- 1 teaspoon ground turmeric
- 1 teaspoon Kashmiri chilli powder
- 1½ tablespoons vegetable or rapeseed (canola) oil
- 50 g (2 oz) pomegranate seeds
- 3 spring onions (scallions), thinly sliced
- ½ bunch of coriander (cilantro), leaves picked and torn
- small handful of mint leaves
- 1 green chilli, thinly sliced
- 1 tablespoon nigella seeds
- sea salt

For the dressing

- 150 g (5 oz) full-fat (whole) Greek yoghurt or soy dairy-free yoghurt
- 3 tablespoons mayonnaise or vegan mayonnaise
- 2 teaspoons mild curry powder
- 2 tablespoons mango chutney
- juice of 2 limes

Trade in the classic, old-school coronation chicken for this fresh and fragrant veggie version (which can easily become vegan) made with spiced roasted wedges of cauliflower, a fresh yoghurt dressing and lots of fresh herbs. The spices are ramped up with the addition of Kashmiri chilli powder and heady garam masala. You can use this sauce in other ways, too. Mix it with chickpeas (garbanzos) or hard-boiled chopped eggs and squish it between sourdough for a delicious vegetarian coronation sandwich.

1. Preheat the oven to 180°C fan (350°F/gas 6). For the dressing, combine all the ingredients in a large bowl. Season with salt and set aside in the fridge.

2. Toast the flaked almonds in a small dry frying pan (skillet) over a medium heat for 5 minutes, or until golden brown. Leave to cool slightly.

3. Sit the cauliflower on a cutting board and cut it into 6 wedges, keeping the leaves attached. Toss the cauliflower and leaves with the garam masala, turmeric, Kashmiri chilli powder, oil and a good pinch of salt in a large mixing bowl. Spread out on to a large baking sheet and and roast for 25–35 minutes until tender; you should be able to pierce it with a cutlery knife.

4. Arrange the cauliflower on a serving platter, then spoon over the yoghurt dressing. Scatter over the toasted almonds, pomegranate seeds, spring onions, coriander, mint, sliced green chilli and nigella seeds, and finish with a little extra salt, if you like. Serve.

Extra ideas

- Garam masala is delicious when roasted with nuts. Try swapping the spices in the Sweet and Salty Cashews recipe on page 176 for 2 tablespoons garam masala.
- **Quick mango and turmeric dip** – mix 150 g (5 oz) thick Greek yoghurt with 1 teaspoon ground turmeric, 2 tablespoons mango chutney, 1 teaspoon nigella seeds and the grated zest and juice of 1 lime. Serve with fried onion rings or poppadums.

Snacks and Sides

Szechuan Pepper Smacked Cucumbers

Szechuan Peppercorns (page 74), **Chilli** (page 32)

Serves 4–5

Takes: 15 mins, plus 30 mins standing
Effort level: Easy

- ¾ teaspoon Szechuan peppercorns
- 2 cucumbers
- 1 teaspoon sea salt
- 2 tablespoons caster (superfine) sugar
- 2 tablespoons dark soy sauce
- 3 tablespoons rice wine vinegar or Chinese black vinegar
- ½ teaspoon chilli (hot pepper) flakes
- 1 fat garlic clove, crushed

Smacked cucumbers take their name from the action of bashing the cucumbers open with a rolling pin to create 'smacked', uneven chunks. They are then tossed in a sweet, salty, vinegar-laden sauce. These cucumbers are perfect eaten alongside dumplings or noodles, or try them with the Spicy Chilli Oil and Cumin Lamb Noodles on page 114.

1. Heat a small dry frying pan (skillet) over a low heat. Add the peppercorns and fry for 3–5 minutes until fragrant. Transfer to a spice grinder or pestle and mortar and grind to a fine powder.

2. Using a rolling pin, lightly bash the cucumbers on a cutting board in several places until they split and break, then chop into chunky pieces. Sprinkle over the salt, then leave to stand in a colander over the sink for 30 minutes.

3. In a large bowl, combine the sugar, soy sauce, vinegar, chilli flakes, garlic and toasted Szechuan peppercorns. Tip in the cucumbers and mix well until combined. Eat immediately or leave to stand in the refrigerator for several days to help develop the flavour.

Quick tips

- Add Szechuan peppercorns to vegetable or meat broths for noodle soups.
- Grind Szechuan peppercorns in a spice grinder or pestle and mortar and add a little at a time to your usual stir-fry recipes.

Roast Squash, Spiced Brown Butter and Feta Yoghurt

Chilli or Pul Biber (pages 32 and 60), **Coriander Seeds** (page 36), **Cumin** (page 40)

Serves 4 as a main or 6 as a side

Takes: 40 mins
Effort level: Easy

- ½ large squash (about 550 g/ 1 lb 4 oz once prepped)
- 2 teaspoons ground cumin
- 1 tablespoon olive oil
- 200 g (7 oz) feta
- 200 g (7 oz) full-fat (whole) Greek yoghurt
- 40 g (1½ oz) unsalted butter
- 1 teaspoon chilli (hot pepper) flakes (Aleppo chilli pepper works well)
- 1 teaspoon coriander seeds
- ½ small bunch of dill, finely chopped
- sea salt

There is something addictive about coriander seeds. Get to know them better: smell them, crush them, toast them lightly until popping in the pan. They are extremely versatile and their taste is fresh, and more citrussy when whole rather than ground. They can be used easily as a finisher or seasoning, adding a warming, aromatic fragrance and a light crunch. Sprinkle them on salads or whisk them into dressings; they are particularly delicious fried in butter. There is something special about the combination of hot, spiced food with cold yoghurt. This recipe for roasted squash and creamy feta yoghurt is simple, but a real go-to combination that you will come back to time and time again. Eat as a main with bread and a grain salad, or have as a side to slow-roasted lamb.

1. Preheat the oven to 200°C fan (400°F/gas 7). Cut the squash in half. Remove the seeds and discard, then slice the flesh into chunky 2–3 cm (¾–1¼ in) half moons. There's no need to peel it.

2. Toss the squash with the cumin, olive oil and a generous sprinkle of sea salt on a large baking sheet, then roast for 30–35 minutes until tender.

3. Meanwhile, add the feta and Greek yoghurt to a food processor and blitz until smooth and creamy. Season with some salt, then spread this on a serving plate.

4. Warm the butter in a frying pan (skillet) over a medium heat for 3–4 minutes until it just begins to smell biscuit brown, then add the chilli flakes and coriander seeds and cook for 20 seconds. Season with a little salt.

5. Pile the squash on to the feta yoghurt, drizzle over the butter and finish with the dill to serve.

Extra ideas

- **Greek Salad** - Make a Greek salad with chopped cucumber, Kalamata olives, big fat chunks of feta and ripe tomatoes, then finish with crushed coriander seeds, mint and dill.
- Add coriander seeds to a cheese scone mixture or soda bread. Coriander seeds and cheese make surprisingly happy companions.

Crispy Curry Leaf Roast Potatoes

Cumin (page 40), **Garam Masala** (page 44), **Turmeric** (page 76), **Chilli** (page 32), **Mustard Seeds** (page 50)

Serves 5–6

Takes: 40 mins
Effort level: Easy

- 500 g (1 lb 2 oz) new potatoes
- 1 tablespoon rapeseed (canola) or olive oil
- ½ teaspoon garam masala
- 1 teaspoon ground turmeric
- ½ teaspoon chilli (hot pepper) flakes
- 1 heaped teaspoon sea salt flakes
- 50 g (2 oz) unsalted butter
- 1 teaspoon black mustard seeds
- 1 teaspoon cumin seeds
- 20 curry leaves
- sea salt

You can quite literally add any spice to a roasted potato and it will taste delicious. In India, the potato dishes are some of the most flavourful; tossing potatoes with Indian spices like turmeric and garam masala works particularly well because they soak up these flavours so beautifully. Nigel Slater has the most moreish and wonderfully spiced recipe for potatoes with turmeric and spinach. This recipe is inspired by said dish, but with crispy smashed potatoes and a delicious curry leaf, tarka-style butter that's poured over the top. If you find a bag of fresh curry leaves, keep them in the freezer and pop them into all sorts of dishes; they have a fantastically fragrant quality that's unbeatable.

1. Preheat the oven to 180°C fan (350°F/gas 6). Bring a large saucepan of well-salted water to the boil. Add the potatoes and cook for 10–12 minutes until a butter knife can be easily inserted into them. Drain and allow to steam-dry for 5 minutes, then tip into a large roasting tin (pan) and lightly bash each potato with the bottom of a heavy-based mug to crush them slightly.

2. Add the oil, garam masala, turmeric, chilli flakes and sea salt flakes and toss to coat, then roast for 20–25 minutes until golden and crispy.

3. Heat the butter in a small frying pan (skillet) over a medium heat. Add the mustard seeds, cumin seeds and curry leaves and cook for 3–4 minutes until the butter is turning golden brown and biscuity and the curry leaves are crispy. Tip the butter over the roasted potatoes and toss together. Serve with yoghurt to dunk, or simply serve the potatoes as a side dish with a fish curry or dhal.

Extra ideas

- Crush the potatoes and spices with a masher and layer on top of a shepherd's or cottage-pie filling for a spicy curry topping.
- Add garam masala to your preferred cornbread recipe, then drizzle with melted butter and fried curry leaves.
- Fry eggs in salted butter, along with curry leaves, turmeric, chilli flakes and mustard seeds until crispy, then pile on to toast.

Spiced Kashmiri Chilli Sweet and Salty Cashews

Chilli (page 32), **Cumin** (page 40), **Amchur** (page 26), **Nigella** (page 51)

Serves 10

Takes: 30 mins
Effort level: Easy

- 30 g (1 oz) unsalted butter
- 3 teaspoons Kashmiri chilli powder
- 3 teaspoons cumin seeds
- 2 teaspoons amchur powder
- 450 g (1 lb/3 cups) cashews
- 50 g (2 oz/2¾ tablespoons) runny honey
- 2 teaspoons nigella seeds
- 1½ tablespoons sea salt flakes

It's important to always have a savoury snack recipe in your repertoire in the event of a last-minute social gathering. Party nuts need a good balance of salt, sweet and spicy; in this case, the sweet is honey and the spicy is a hit of Kashmiri chilli powder, cumin and amchur. These cashews are so moreish and very hard to stop eating once you start, but in the unlikely case you do have leftovers, store them in an airtight jar for up to two weeks.

1. Preheat the oven to 160°C fan (320°F/gas 4).

2. Melt the butter in a roomy frying pan (skillet) over a medium heat until foaming. Add the chilli, cumin and amchur and cook for 1 minute.

3. Tip the nuts into a large bowl. Toss through the spiced butter, honey, nigella seeds and salt, then spread them on to a large baking sheet. Roast for 20–25 minutes, turning every so often. Remove from the oven and shake the baking sheet well before leaving to cool completely. Store in a jar and eat alongside an ice-cold beer.

Extra ideas

- **Grilled tomatoes with Kashmiri chilli and butter** – Toss 500 g (1 lb 2 oz) cherry tomatoes in a bowl with 1 tablespoon Kashmiri chilli powder, 2 teaspoons nigella seeds, 5 fresh curry leaves, 50 g (2 oz) unsalted butter and 1 teaspoon sea salt. Grill (broil) under a grill (broiler) preheated to high for 5–10 minutes until juicy and popping. Serve piled on toast or as a side dish.
- Sprinkle nigella seeds on cooked white rice or couscous.
- Nigella seeds add a gentle oniony bite to fresh salads. Whisk them into a dressing or sprinkle on a summer tomato and mint salad.
- **Cucumber, lime and nigella salad** – Toss 2 teaspoons nigella seeds with 1 chopped cucumber, the juice of 1 lime and 2 tablespoons toasted sesame oil. Finish with lots of sea salt and leave to stand for 30 minutes before eating.

HOPADELIC

Deli Pickles

Coriander (page 36), **Peppercorns** (page 58), **Mustard Seeds** (page 50)

Makes 2 litre (70 fl oz) jar

Takes: 30 mins, plus 48 hours pickling
Effort level: A little effort

- 1 tablespoon mustard seeds
- 2 teaspoons coriander seeds, crushed
- 2 teaspoons black peppercorns
- 500 ml (17 fl oz/2 cups) white wine vinegar
- 700 ml (24 fl oz/scant 3 cups) water
- 2 tablespoons sea salt
- 7 tablespoons caster (superfine) sugar
- 1 kg (2 lb 4 oz) baby cucumbers, halved lengthways
- small bunch of dill, torn

A jar of dill pickles is a welcome addition to any refrigerator or store cupboard. Homemade are definitely best in this case, and a good blend of aromatics like mustard seeds, coriander seeds and peppercorns makes all the difference. Use the small Turkish cucumbers if you can find them, as they have a good crunch and are just the right size to fit in a Kilner or mason jar. If you can't find any, thickly slice the same weight of ordinary cucumbers. Once pickled, they are good for squishing into burgers, layering up on a pastrami sandwich or eating straight out of the jar.

1. Toast the mustard seeds, coriander seeds and black peppercorns in a dry frying pan (skillet) over a medium heat for 5 minutes.

2. Heat the vinegar, water, salt, sugar and toasted spices in a large saucepan over a medium heat , swirling the pan gently until the sugar and salt have dissolved.

3. Wash the cucumbers thoroughly and pack them into a large, sterilised 2 litre (70 fl oz) Kilner jar or 2 × 1 litre (34 fl oz) jars. Pour over the hot pickling liquid and leave to cool for 15 minutes with the lid(s) open, then seal and leave to pickle at room temperature for 24 hours. Transfer to the refrigerator and eat within a week.

Extra ideas

- Add mustard seeds to a homemade chutney recipe. They work well in an apple or apricot chutney, cutting through the sweet flavours.
- Shred Brussels sprouts or cabbage and fry them in butter with caraway and yellow mustard seeds for a punchy side dish to roast pork or sausages.

Kimchi Togarashi Dip

Shichimi Togarashi (page 66)

Serves 6

Takes: 10 mins
Effort level: Easy

- 100 g (3½ oz) kimchi, drained and finely chopped
- 2 spring onions (scallions), finely chopped
- 150 g (5 oz/⅔ cup) sour cream
- 180 g (6 oz) cream cheese
- 1–2 teaspoons sriracha sauce
- juice of ½ small lemon
- 1 teaspoon shichimi togarashi, plus extra for sprinkling

To serve
- cucumber batons
- crisps (chips)
- crackers

There are few things as satisfying as a creamy dip surrounded by an array of delicious vessels for scooping. Originating from Hawaii, the cheesy kimchi dip combines cream cheese, sour cream and Korean kimchi, with the extra addition of Japan's shichimi togarashi spice blend, which cuts through the creamy, vinegary flavours. It's also great spread on bread or squished into a burger.

1. Tip the kimchi into a large bowl with the spring onions. In a separate bowl, beat together the sour cream and cream cheese with a whisk until smooth. Add this to the kimchi and spring onions, along with the sriracha, lemon juice and shichimi togarashi, and mix everything together. Season to taste with a little salt.

2. Spoon the dip into a bowl, sprinkle with extra togarashi and serve with cucumbers, crisps and crackers.

Extra ideas

- Try mixing 200 g (7 oz) yoghurt of your choice with some salt, a spoonful of hot sauce and a pinch of shichimi togarashi for a super-speedy version of this dip.
- Sprinkle shichimi togarashi on thickly sliced cucumber and tomatoes with a little salt and oil.
- Cook some udon noodles and toss them with shichimi togarashi, butter and soy sauce for a quick dinner.

Chilli and Honey Fried Halloumi

Pul Biber (page 60)

Serves 2–4

Takes: 10 mins
Effort level: Easy

- ½ tablespoon olive oil
- 220 g (73/4 oz) block halloumi, thickly sliced
- 2 tablespoons clear runny honey
- 1 tablespoon chilli (hot pepper) flakes (Aleppo or Urfa chilli pepper work well)

Sweet, salty and hot are three things that make for something totally delicious. Halloumi teams well with honey and chilli because of its intensely salty flavour. Eat this as part of a wider meal or mezze with flatbreads, hummus, olives, baba ghanoush, or whatever you fancy. It's also great tossed in a tabbouleh salad. My preferred chilli with this is Urfa, because it has a smoky, burnt tone to it, but any dried chilli will do. You could also use za'atar or sumac, if you prefer.

1. Heat the oil in a large frying pan over a medium-high heat.

2. Pat the halloumi with paper towels to remove any excess liquid, then add the halloumi to the pan and cook for 2–3 minutes on each side until golden brown.

3. Drizzle the honey over the halloumi and cook for a further 1 minute. Scatter over the chilli and serve.

Extra ideas

- **Baked feta with honey and chilli** – The same idea can be used when baking feta. Simply preheat the oven to 160°C fan (320°F/gas 4). Add the feta to a baking dish and drizzle it with the oil. Add the honey and chilli and bake for 30–35 minutes until golden and sticky.
- **Spiced cheese board** - Mix Urfa or Aleppo chilli pepper with honey and drizzle it over cheese on your cheese board. This works really well with young pecorino, Comté or a soft, young goat's cheese.

Something Sweet, Something Baked

Spiced Rum Sticky Toffee Pudding

Allspice (page 24), **Cinnamon** (page 34), **Ginger** (page 48)

Serves 6–8

Takes: 1 hr, plus 30 mins soaking
Effort level: Easy

- 50 g (2 oz) unsalted butter, plus extra for greasing
- 250 g (9 oz/1⅓ cups) pitted dates, chopped
- 150 ml (5 fl oz/⅔ cup) boiling water
- 2 tablespoons treacle (blackstrap molasses)
- 175 g (6 oz/generous ¾ cup) soft light brown sugar
- 2 eggs, lightly beaten
- 200 g (7 oz/1⅔ cups) self-raising (self-rising) flour
- 1 teaspoon ground allspice
- 1 teaspoon ground cinnamon
- 1 teaspoon ground ginger
- ¼ nutmeg, finely grated
- 1 teaspoon bicarbonate of soda (baking soda)
- ¼ teaspoon sea salt
- vanilla ice cream, thick cream or cold pouring cream, to serve

For the sauce
- 50 g (2 oz) unsalted butter
- 2 tablespoons treacle (blackstrap molasses)
- 1 teaspoon vanilla bean paste
- 75 g (2½ oz) soft light brown sugar
- 300 ml (10 fl oz/1¼cups) double (heavy) cream
- 3 tablespoons dark spiced rum

Here, the classic sticky toffee pudding is elevated by spices and a rich, deep golden rum caramel, creating a dessert inspired by a British classic and the spicing of a sticky Jamaican black cake often eaten at Christmas. Bake it until golden and risen, then smother it in a golden caramel sauce before eating with plenty of cream.

1. Preheat the oven to 160°C fan/320°F/gas 4 and grease a medium-sized baking dish with butter. Add the dates to a large heatproof bowl, cover with the boiling water and leave to soak for 30 minutes, then blitz the dates and soaking liquid in a food processor to a smooth purée.

2. In a large bowl, beat together the butter, treacle, sugar and eggs, then fold in the flour, spices, bicarbonate of soda and salt, followed by the date purée. Spoon into the prepared dish.

3. Bake for 40–50 minutes (checking after 40 minutes), or until risen and firm to the touch.

4. While the pudding is baking, make the sauce. Tip the butter, treacle, vanilla, sugar and cream into a saucepan and cook over a medium heat for 4–5 minutes, stirring, until the sugar dissolves. Increase the heat to high and bubble for 3 minutes, then whisk in a pinch of salt and the rum.

5. When you're ready to serve, reheat the sauce and pour it over the pudding. Serve with ice cream, thick cream or cold pouring cream.

Extra ideas

- Add allspice to baked fruit, like apples, quince and pears, or to the topping of a crumble.
- Use allspice in the batter of cakes like a sticky ginger cake or fruity flapjack.

Grapefruit and Szechuan Ricciarelli (Italian Biscuits)

Szechuan Peppercorns (page 74)

Makes 15

Takes: 50 mins, plus overnight chilling
Effort level: A little effort

- ½ teaspoon Szechuan peppercorns
- 2 egg whites
- 200 g (7 oz/1⅔ cups) icing (confectioners') sugar, plus extra for dusting
- ½ teaspoon baking powder
- grated zest of 1 large pink grapefruit
- 200 g (7 oz/2 cups) ground almonds
- ¼ teaspoon fine sea salt
- 30 g (1 oz/⅓ cup) flaked (flaked) almonds

Spices and almonds have always sat well together. Whether you add cardamom to a frangipane or cover a spiced Christmas cake with a blanket of marzipan, they complement each other immensely. These little almond-based Italian biscuits (cookies) originated in Sienna. They have a chewy texture and a crispy exterior, and are wonderful wrapped up for Christmas. The Szechuan and grapefruit in this recipe create citrus and floral notes, but if you find Szechuan a little controversial then ground cardamom or crushed fennel seeds work beautifully as well.

1. Toast the Szechuan peppercorns in a small, dry frying pan (skillet) over a medium heat for 5 minutes, then grind into a fine powder in a spice grinder or pestle and mortar. Set aside.

2. Whisk the egg whites in a large bowl with an electric hand-held whisk on a high speed until you have stiff peaks. Alternatively, use a stand mixer fitted with a whisk attachment. Using a spatula, fold in the icing sugar, baking powder, grapefruit zest, ground almonds and salt until you have a thick, sticky batter. Cover and chill in the refrigerator for 12–24 hours.

3. The next day, preheat the oven to 140°C fan (280°F/gas 3) and line 2 baking sheets with baking parchment. Dust a work surface liberally with icing sugar, then roll the dough out into a 13 cm (5 in) long sausage. Cut the sausage into 15 evenly sized pieces, then form each one into an oval shape with your hands. Arrange on the prepared baking sheets, cut-side down, then gently press some flaked almonds into the top of each one. Bake for 20 minutes.

4. Leave the cookies to cool on the baking sheets (they will seem very soft when they first come out, but they harden up when left to cool) Once cool, dust with extra icing sugar. Store in an airtight container for up to 5 days.

Extra ideas

- Crush ¼ teaspoon Szechuan peppercorns and add to a glass of Prosecco, along with some fresh grapefruit juice.
- Mix caster (superfine) sugar with Szechuan peppercorns and sprinkle it on a fruit salad.
- Fold 2 teaspoons ground Szechuan peppercorns into a meringue or pavlova base before baking. Serve with poached pears or berries.

Apple, Cardamom and Custard Doughnuts

Cardamom (page 28)

Makes 15

Takes: 2 hrs, plus 1 hr 30 mins rising and proving
Effort level: A weekend challenge

- 130 ml (4/2fl oz/½ cup) full-fat (whole) milk
- 500 g (1 lb 2 oz/4 cups) strong white bread flour
- 70 g (2½ oz/⅓ cup) golden caster (superfine) sugar
- ¾ teaspoon fine sea salt
- 2 × 7 g (¼ oz) fast-action dried yeast
- 3 medium eggs, lightly beaten
- 120 g (4 oz) unsalted butter, softened and cubed
- vegetable oil, for oiling and deep-frying

For the custard

- 200 ml (7 fl oz/scant 1 cup) full-fat (whole) milk
- 150 ml (5 fl oz/⅔ cup) double (heavy) cream
- 1 vanilla pod (bean), halved longthways and seeds scraped out
- 3 egg yolks
- 50 g (2 oz/scant ¼ cup) caster (superfine) sugar
- 2 tablespoons cornflour (cornstarch)

Scandinavia has one of the highest consumption rates of cardamom outside of Asia and the Arab world. It is presented in the form of cakes, cookies and a famous knotted, sweetened bun named *kardemummabullar*. This recipe is inspired by the pairing of an enriched dough with crushed cardamom, and presents itself in the form of a deep-fried fluffy doughnut. Spiked with a cardamom sugar, spiced apple sauce and perfectly wobbly custard, these weekend sweet treats will awaken nostalgia, and are definitely worth a little effort and a few hours of your time.

1. To make the dough, pour the milk into a large saucepan and slowly heat over a low heat. Once it begins to steam, remove from the heat and pour into a measuring jug. If it has reduced, top up to 130 ml (4½ fl oz/½ cup) with extra milk, then leave to cool until tepid.

2. Add the flour to a stand mixer fitted with a hook attachment and stir through the golden caster (superfine) sugar, salt and yeast with a spoon. Begin mixing on low speed to combine the dry ingredients, then add the tepid milk and eggs and keep mixing for 10 minutes, or until you have a smooth, elastic dough. Still mixing, gradually add cubes of the softened butter to the dough. When all the butter has been added, continue mixing for a further 5–6 minutes until the butter is well incorporated and the dough is sticky and stretchy.

3. Lightly oil a large bowl, then transfer the dough to the bowl. Cover and leave in a warm place for 1 hour, or until doubled in size.

4. Lightly oil 2 large baking sheets. Divide the risen dough into 15 equal-sized pieces, weighing for accuracy, if you like (they should be about 62 g/2 oz each). Roll the dough pieces into balls and place them on the prepared baking sheets, spaced well apart. Cover with lightly oiled baking parchment or a light dish towel (if it's too heavy, it will keep the dough from rising) and leave to prove in a warm place for 25–30 minutes until doubled in size.

continues overleaf

For the apple filling

- 2 large Bramley (cooking) apples (350 g/12 oz), peeled and cut into 5 mm (¼ in) cubes
- 80 g (3 oz/generous ⅓ cup) caster (superfine) sugar
- 100 ml (3½ fl oz/scant ½ cup) water
- 12 cardamom pods, bashed

For the coating

- 150 g (5 oz/⅔ cup) caster (superfine) sugar
- 1 tablespoon ground cardamom or the ground seeds of 6 cardamom pods

5. Line 1–2 large baking sheets with paper towels and set aside. Fill a medium-sized, heavy-based saucepan two-thirds full of vegetable oil and place over a low–medium heat, bringing the temperature up to 165°C (329°F) on a cooking thermometer (or test by adding a small piece of dough to the oil – if it sizzles and rises to the surface immediately, the temperature is correct). Working in batches of about 3 at a time, carefully lift the doughnuts and gently lower into the hot oil. Deep-fry each batch for 6 minutes, turning halfway through, until golden brown. Remove with a slotted spoon and transfer to the prepared baking sheets while you cook the other batches. Leave to cool completely.

6. For the custard, heat the milk, cream and vanilla seeds together in a saucepan over a low heat until just steaming. Whisk together the egg yolks and caster sugar in a large heatproof bowl, then sift in the cornflour and mix well until it forms a smooth paste. Add the milk slowly to the egg mixture, whisking constantly, then pour the custard back into the pan and bring to a simmer, whisking until thickened. Remove from the heat and leave to cool to room temperature. Once cooled, spoon into a piping (pastry) bag fitted with a metal tip. Set aside.

7. For the apple filling, tip the chopped apples, caster sugar, water and cardamom pods into a small saucepan. Bring to a simmer and cook gently for 10–12 minutes until the apples are soft and broken down. Set aside to cool, then remove and discard the cardamom pods. Spoon into another piping bag fitted with a round piping nozzle and set aside.

8. For the coating, mix together the caster sugar and ground cardamom in a shallow bowl, then roll the doughnuts in the sugar until lightly coated. Make a hole in the side of each doughnut with a metal skewer, then pipe a little of the apple filling into each doughnut, followed by the custard. Serve.

Extra ideas

- Swap the cardamom for 1 tablespoon ground cinnamon in the apple sauce and 2 teaspoons ground cinnamon in the sugar coating for a wintery spiced apple take on these doughnuts.
- **Easy cardamom, plum and ricotta cake** – Preheat the oven to 170°C fan (340°F/gas 5). Grease the base and sides of a 20 cm (8 in) springform round cake tin (pan) with butter and line the base with a disc of baking parchment. Tip 250 g (9 oz) ricotta and 230 g (8 oz/1 cup) golden caster (superfine) sugar into a large bowl and beat together with an electric hand-held whisk for 5 minutes. Beat in 3 eggs, followed by 150 g (5 oz) melted and cooled unsalted butter. Fold in 180 g (6 oz/scant 1½ cups) self-raising (self-rising) flour, ½ teaspoon baking powder, ½ teaspoon salt and the crushed seeds from 6 cardamom pods. Spoon into the prepared tin and press in 3–4 halved and pitted plums or apricots. Bake for 50–60 minutes until risen and golden brown. Leave to cool, then dust with icing (confectioners') sugar.

White Chocolate, Espresso and Cardamom Cookies

Cardamom (page 28)

Makes 12

Takes: 35 mins, plus 30 mins chilling
Effort level: A little effort

- 10 green cardamom pods
- 120 g (4 oz) unsalted butter, softened
- 80 g (3 oz/scant ½ cup) soft light brown sugar
- 60 g (2 oz/¼ cup) golden caster (superfine) sugar
- 1 tablespoon instant espresso powder
- 3 egg yolks
- 1 teaspoon vanilla bean paste
- 100 g (3½ oz/generous ¾ cup) plain (all-purpose) flour
- 80 g (3 oz/generous ¾ cup) wholemeal rye flour
- ½ teaspoon sea salt flakes, plus extra for sprinkling (optional)
- ½ teaspoon bicarbonate of soda (baking soda)
- ½ teaspoon baking powder
- 150 g (5 oz) white chocolate, chopped into rough chunks

These cookies are inspired by the centuries-old method of making Turkish coffee – which is distinctively strong, dark and often flavoured with cardamom pods. The inclusion of sweet white chocolate offers a wonderful contrasting flavour to the coffee. Add chopped pistachios or walnuts to the cookie batter if you like, but the simplicity of these aromatic flavours together is lovely as it is.

1. Bash open the cardamom pods in a pestle and mortar to release the black seeds, then grind them to a coarse powder.

2. In a stand mixer fitted with a whisk attachment, or with an electric hand-held whisk in a large bowl, beat together the butter and sugars at a medium speed for 5 minutes, or until well combined but not too aerated. Add the coffee, egg yolks and vanilla and mix again. Add the cardamom, flours, salt, bicarbonate of soda, baking powder and chocolate, and mix briefly to combine.

3. Line 2 large baking sheets with baking parchment. Scoop the cookie dough into 12 nuggets, weighing for accuracy if you like (they should be about 50 g/2 oz each). Roll each one into a neat ball. Space them well apart on the lined baking sheets and chill in the refrigerator for 30 minutes. Meanwhile, preheat the oven to 180°C fan (350°F/gas 6).

4. Bake for 10–12 minutes, then leave to cool completely on the baking sheets. Sprinkle with a little extra salt, if you like. These will store well in an airtight container for up to 3 days.

Extra ideas

- Add cardamom to your favourite coffee and walnut cake recipes. The seeds of 7 pods, crushed and added to the dry ingredients, will work really well.
- Cardamom also pairs well with rich, dark chocolate flavours, so add it to brownies with chopped pistachios or a triple chocolate cake.
- Cardamom and pear is a lovely combination; add the seeds to a pear crumble or poach pears in a sugar syrup infused with cardamom.

Spiced Molasses Banana Cake and Cream Cheese Frosting

Allspice (page 24), **Cinnamon** (page 34), **Ginger** (page 48), **Nutmeg** (page 52)

Serves 10

Takes: 1 hr 10 mins
Effort level: A little effort

- 150 g (5 oz) unsalted butter, melted and cooled, plus extra for greasing
- 4 very ripe large bananas (about 450–500 g/1 lb–1 lb 2 oz peeled weight), mashed until smooth
- 130 g (3½ oz/¾ cup) soft light brown sugar
- 50 g (2 oz/2½ tablespoons) molasses or treacle (blackstrap molasses)
- 2 eggs
- 50 g (2 oz/scant ⅓ cup) sour cream
- 200 g (7 oz/1⅔ cups) plain (all-purpose) flour
- 2 teaspoons ground cinnamon
- ½ teaspoon ground ginger
- ½ teaspoon allspice
- ½ teaspoon ground nutmeg
- 1 teaspoon baking powder
- 1 teaspoon bicarbonate of soda (baking soda)
- ½ teaspoon sea salt

For the frosting
- 200 g (7 oz/1⅔ cups) icing (confectioners') sugar
- 100 g (3½ oz) unsalted butter, softened
- 165 g (5¾ oz/¾ cup) cream cheese, at room temperature

This recipe, with its gentle spicing and injection of molasses, is not dissimilar in texture and flavour to a dark and sticky Jamaican ginger cake. Creamy banana and sweet cinnamon are a good match, and the kick of allspice really brings out the banana flavour, while the cream cheese frosting takes it from an everyday bake to a spectacular one. Make it for a friend who needs cheering up or push candles into it for a birthday; it's the kind of bake that brings a smile to your face.

1. Preheat the oven to 180°C fan (350°F/gas 6). Grease the base and sides of a 20 cm (8 in) deep springform cake tin (pan) with butter. Line the base with a round disc of baking parchment.

2. Mash your bananas with a fork until smooth or blitz gently with a hand-held blender to remove any noticeable lumps. In a large bowl, whisk together the mashed banana, butter, sugar, molasses or treacle, eggs and sour cream. Add the flour, cinnamon, ginger, allspice, nutmeg, baking powder, bicarbonate of soda and sea salt to the wet ingredients and whisk until just combined. Tip the batter into the prepared tin and bake for 45–50 minutes until firm to the touch and a skewer inserted into the middle comes out clean. Remove from the oven and leave to cool completely in the tin.

3. For the frosting, in a stand mixer fitted with a whisk attachment or with an electric hand-held whisk in a large bowl, beat together the icing sugar and softened butter at a medium speed for 5–10 minutes until pale in colour and fluffy in texture. Add the cream cheese and beat for another 1 minute.

4. Tip the cooled cake upside down on to a serving plate and top with thick billows of the cream cheese frosting. This will keep in the refrigerator for up to 3 days, but it's doubtful it will last that long.

Try this

- **Baked bananas with maple, rum and cinnamon** – Preheat the oven to 200°C fan (400°F/gas 7). Halve 6 bananas and top them with 1 tablespoon unsalted butter, 2 tablespoons maple syrup, 2 tablespoons dark soft brown sugar, 3–4 tablespoons spiced rum and 2 teaspoons ground cinnamon. Bake for 15 minutes, then serve with vanilla ice cream.

Strawberry and Fennel Seed Ice Cream

Fennel (page 42)

Serves 6–8

Takes: 1 hr, plus 12 hrs freezing
Effort level: A weekend challenge

- ½ quantity of Macerated Strawberries with Fennel Seeds (page 98)
- 300 ml (10 fl oz/1¼ cups) double (heavy) cream
- 300 ml (10 fl oz/1¼ cups) full-fat (whole) milk
- 6 egg yolks
- 200 g (7 oz/generous ¾ cup) caster (superfine) sugar

Strawberries sing of the first wisp of British summertime, and what better way to use up a glut than churning it into a batch of ice cream? The combination of a silky strawberry ice cream and the fragrant hit of liquorice fennel is a real treat. Swap out strawberries for raspberries or stewed gooseberries, if you like. This ice cream is best churned in an ice-cream machine, but if you don't have one, see step 4 below.

1. Blitz the Macerated Strawberries in a food processor to form a purée, then set aside.

2. Warm the cream and milk together in a medium-sized saucepan over a low heat until the mixture begins to steam.

3. In a large heatproof bowl, beat together the egg yolks and sugar with a whisk until slightly thickened. Slowly whisk the milk mixture into the eggs and sugar in a continuous stream. Once incorporated, pour it back into the saucepan and set it over a low heat. Cook gently, stirring constantly, for around 10 minutes, scraping the bottom of the pan as you go. The mixture will gently thicken into a custard – when it's ready, it will coat the back of a spoon. Set the bowl of custard over a bowl of iced water and stir constantly until the custard has cooled. Mix the custard with most of the strawberry purée.

4. Churn the custard in an ice-cream maker, following the manufacturer's instructions. Alternatively, pour the custard into a freezerproof container and freeze for 3 hours, removing the container once every hour and blitzing in a food processor. Then freeze again until firm.

5. When the ice cream is frozen, but not too hard, transfer it into a freezerproof container and swirl in the remaining purée. Cover with a lid or some cling film (plastic wrap) and leave in the freezer overnight before serving. Serve in small bowls or ice-cream cones.

Quick tips

- Try adding bashed fennel seeds to other ice-cream recipes. Citrussy flavours work well with fennel, as do peach, apricot and white chocolate.

No-bake Salted Ginger Caramel Chocolate Tart

Ginger (page 48)

Serves 10

Takes: 1 hr 30 mins, plus 4 hrs 30 mins chilling
Effort level: A little effort

For the base
- 80 g (3 oz) unsalted butter, melted, plus extra for greasing
- 300 g (10½ oz) dark chocolate biscuits (cookies)
- 30 g (1 oz/scant ¼ cup) blanched hazelnuts
- 2 tablespoons cocoa (unsweetened chocolate) powder, plus extra for dusting
- 1 tablespoon ground ginger

For the caramel
- 75 g (2½ oz) unsalted butter
- 75 g (2½ oz/scant ½ cup) soft brown muscovado sugar
- 75 g (2½ fl oz/5 tablespoons) double (heavy) cream
- 1 teaspoon ground ginger
- ½ teaspoon sea salt flakes, plus extra for sprinkling

For the chocolate ganache
- 200 ml (7 fl oz/scant 1 cup) double (heavy) cream
- 150 g (5 oz) good-quality dark chocolate, with at least 70% cocoa solids
- 2 tablespoons golden (light corn) syrup

To serve
- crème fraîche

This tart is unique in that it doesn't require any baking, making it a great go-to entertaining recipe that can be prepared in advance. Its star is a thick layer of ginger salted caramel and a just-set, buttery chocolate ganache. The ground ginger adds just enough warmth to mellow the sweet caramel and rich chocolate topping. Use a good-quality chocolate if you can, as it makes all the difference – and, of course, a good-quality ground ginger.

1. Grease the base of a shallow 20 cm (8 in) springform sandwich cake tin (pan) and line with a disc of baking parchment. Tip the biscuits, nuts and cocoa into a food processor and grind to a medium-coarse, sandy texture. Add the butter and ginger and blitz briefly until the mixture clumps together. Push the mixture into the base of the prepared tin and freeze for 30 minutes.

2. To make the caramel, place the butter, sugar, cream, ginger and salt into a medium-sized saucepan and simmer over a medium heat, stirring, until the sugar dissolves. Increase the heat and bring to the boil. Remove from the heat, pour into the case and freeze for a further 1 hour.

3. For the ganache, heat the cream in a large saucepan over a low heat until steaming. Combine the chocolate and golden syrup in a large heatproof bowl. Pour the hot cream over them, whisking constantly until the chocolate has melted. Pour this mixture over the caramel, then sprinkle with salt flakes and leave to set in the refrigerator for 3 hours.

4. When ready to eat, push the tart out of its tin. Place on a plate and leave to come to room temperature for 30–40 minutes. Serve sliced with a dollop of crème fraiche. The tart will keep in the refrigerator for up to 3 days.

Extra ideas

- Add 2 teaspoons ground ginger to a chocolate cake recipe for a warming, spicy edge.
- Find your favourite mince pie recipe in the festive season and add 1½ teaspoons ground ginger to the pastry or mincemeat filling.
- **Apple, ginger and Calvados crumble** – Make your favourite apple crumble recipe, and add 2 teaspoons ground ginger to the crumble topping and 50 ml (1¾ fl oz/3 tablespoons) Calvados to the apple filling.

Spiced Pumpkin Tres Leches Cake

Cinnamon (page 34), **Nutmeg** (page 52)

Serves 12

Takes: 50 mins, plus 30 mins cooling and 9 hrs chilling
Effort level: A little effort

- 120 g (4 oz) unsalted butter, melted, plus extra for greasing
- 5 eggs
- ½ teaspoon fine salt
- 225 g (8 oz/scant 1 cup) caster (superfine) sugar
- 200 g (7 oz) tinned pumpkin purée
- 250 g (9 oz/2 cups) self-raising (self-rising) flour
- 2 teaspoons baking powder
- 1 teaspoon ground cinnamon
- ½ nutmeg, finely grated
- ½ teaspoon mixed spice
- 400 g (14 oz) tin condensed milk
- 400 g (14 oz) tin evaporated milk

For the topping

- 300 g (10 fl oz/1¼ cups) double (heavy) cream
- 2 tablespoons icing (confectioners') sugar
- 4 tablespoons tinned pumpkin purée
- nutmeg, for grating

Tres leches means three milks, and this bake is all about the soaking. The sponge is thick and fluffy in texture and moist from the sweet milks of its name, and it is topped with a crown of lightly whipped cream. The gentle addition of pumpkin pie spices as well as nutty pumpkin purée makes it extra special. It's great for a celebration, as it can be made in advance. You can bake it 1–2 days before serving and leave it in the refrigerator, before bringing it to the table and cutting into big slices, awaiting the smiles upon your guests' faces.

1. Preheat the oven to 160°C fan (320°F/gas 4). Grease and line the base and sides of a deep 23 × 23 cm (9 × 9 in) square cake tin (pan).

2. Separate the egg whites and yolks into 2 large clean bowls. Using an electric hand-held whisk, whisk the egg whites and salt together at a high speed until soft peaks form, adding 50 g (2 oz/scant ¼ cup) of the sugar, 1 tablespoon at a time, until well incorporated. Alternatively, use a stand mixer fitted with a whisk attachment.

3. In a separate bowl, using a balloon whisk, whisk together the egg yolks, remaining sugar and melted butter for 5 minutes, or until lighter in colour and thickened. Add the pumpkin purée, flour, baking powder, cinnamon, nutmeg and mixed spice. Stir in a large spoonful of the egg whites to loosen, then gently fold through the remaining egg whites with a large metal spoon or spatula, being careful not to knock out too much of the air. Spoon the batter into the prepared cake tin and bake in the centre of the oven for 35 minutes, or until risen and firm to the touch.

4. Mix together the condensed milk and evaporated milk in a large bowl. Prick holes all over the warm cake with a cocktail stick (toothpick), then pour the soaking mixture over the cake. Leave to cool, still in the tin, at room temperature for 30 minutes, then cover and chill in the refrigerator overnight.

5. The next day, make the topping. In a large bowl, whip together the cream, icing sugar, 2 tablespoons of the pumpkin purée and a good grating of nutmeg. Spoon and swirl the cream on top of the cake, then dot with the remaining pumpkin purée and ripple this through with the back of a spoon. Chill in the refrigerator for 1 hour. Serve in thick slices, straight out of the tin.

PX Sherry and Star Anise Roasted Plum Yoghurt Cream Pavlova

Star Anise (page 68)

Serves 8–10

Takes: 3 hrs 30 mins, plus overnight cooling
Effort level: A weekend challenge

- 4 egg whites
- 120 g (4 oz/⅔ cup) light brown soft sugar
- 100 g (3½ oz/scant ½ cup) caster (superfine) sugar
- ½ teaspoon white wine vinegar
- 1 teaspoon cornflour (cornstarch)
- ½ teaspoon cream of tartar
- sea salt

For the topping

- 10 large plums, halved and pitted
- 100 g (3½ oz/½ cup) soft brown sugar
- 3 star anise
- 100 ml (3½ fl oz/scant ½ cup) Pedro Ximinez sherry, port or red wine
- 250 g (9 oz) mascarpone
- 100 g (3½ oz/½ cup) light muscovado sugar
- 1 tablespoon vanilla bean paste
- 450 g (1 lb) thick Greek yoghurt (the thickest you can find)

When plums are roasted, something magical happens: they release a rich, wine-like ruby-red syrup that can be poured on to desserts such as pavlova. Stone fruits and spices work really well together, and anise, with its liquorice and smoky notes particularly complements plums. The thick, billowy combination of yoghurt and mascarpone cuts through the sweet, boozy plums and crisp pavlova, making it a wonderful late summer or autumnal (fall) dessert. In the winter, try swapping the plums for halved figs or roasted seasonal apples; in the summer, use roast, pitted cherries in the same way.

1. Preheat the oven to 100°C fan (210°F/gas ½). Using a plate as a guide, draw a 22 cm (8½ in) circle on a sheet of baking parchment, then flip over on to a large baking sheet.

2. Beat the egg whites in a clean bowl with an electric hand-held whisk until soft peaks form. Alternatively, use a stand mixer fitted with a whisk attachment. While still whisking, gradually add both of the sugars, 1–2 tablespoons at a time, until the mixture is thick and glossy. Whisk for a further 5 minutes, then whisk in a pinch of salt, along with the vinegar, cornflour and cream of tartar. Dollop the meringue into the centre of the circle on the baking parchment, spreading it to the edge of the circle using a spatula or palette knife and creating a dip in the centre. Bake on the lower shelf of the oven for 2 hours 30 minutes–3 hours, then turn off the oven and leave the meringue to cool inside it for at least 6 hours, or overnight.

3. The next day, remove the meringue from the oven. For the topping, preheat the oven to 180°C fan (350°F/gas 6). Arrange the plums, cut-side down, in a roasting dish. Sprinkle over the light brown sugar, star anise and sherry, and roast for 15–20 minutes until the plums are tender but still holding their shape. Leave to cool completely. In a large bowl, whisk together the mascarpone, muscovado sugar and vanilla until the sugar has dissolved, then gently fold through the yoghurt. (If the mixture is a little thin, chill it for 2 hours, or until thickened.)

4. Pile the mascarpone mixture on top of the meringue. Remove the star anise from the plums and discard, then pile the plums on top of the mascarpone, drizzling with any of the lovely syrupy juices left in the bottom of the dish. Serve. Store in the refrigerator for up to 3 days.

Creamy Rice Pudding with Cardamom Peaches

Cardamom (page 28)

Serves 4–6

Takes: 1 hr, plus 3 hrs chilling (optional)
Effort level: Easy

- 175 g (6 oz/¾ cup) pudding or short-grain rice
- 900 ml (30 fl oz/3¾ cups) full-fat (whole) milk, plus an extra 150 ml (5 fl oz/⅔ cup) if needed
- 150 ml (5 fl oz/⅔ cup) double (heavy) cream
- 85 g (3 oz/⅓ cup) caster (superfine) sugar
- 1 teaspoon vanilla bean paste

For the peaches
- 4 large ripe peaches, pitted and each sliced into 6 wedges
- 10 cardamom pods, bashed
- 100 g (3½ oz/½ cup) soft light brown sugar
- juice of 1 lemon
- 1 teaspoon cornflour (cornstarch)

There is a small window of time in the summer when peaches take centre stage and become one of the most delicious fruits you can buy from the greengrocer or supermarket. Making them even more delicious here is the introduction of cardamom; its heady fragrance brings out the perfumed sweetness in these stone fruits. These lightly poached peaches, sitting atop a bed of creamy rice pudding, make a perfect dessert. Eat the rice pudding warm or cold for those hotter summer days. For other stone fruit and cardamom ideas, try the Cardamom-poached Apricots on page 89.

1. Tip the peaches into a large saucepan over a low heat. Add the cardamom pods, light brown sugar and lemon juice, and bring to a low simmer. Cover with a lid and cook over a low heat for 5 minutes, or until syrupy. Pour a little of the syrup into a cup and mix with the cornflour. Pour this back into the pan and gently stir, then bring the mixture back to a simmer for several minutes. Remove the pan from the heat and leave to cool, then chill in the refrigerator until ready to serve.

2. Wash the rice in a sieve (fine mesh strainer) under cold running water for 5 minutes, or until the water runs clear. Add to a large saucepan with the 900 ml (30 fl oz/3¾ cups) milk, along with the cream, caster sugar and vanilla. Cook over a low heat for 35–40 minutes, stirring frequently, until the rice is just cooked through. Once the rice is cooked, remove from the heat. You can now serve this warm or leave to cool, then transfer to the refrigerator and leave for a minimum of 2 hours or until cold. If left to cool, stir the extra 150 ml (5 fl oz/⅔ cup) milk into the rice to loosen when ready to serve.

3. To serve, scoop out the cardamom pods from the peaches and discard, then serve the rice pudding in bowls, topped with the peaches.

Extra ideas

- Try this recipe with fresh strawberries, or apples and pears in the cooler winter months.
- Add bashed cardamom pods to homemade apricot jam.
- Add the seeds of 5 cardamom pods to a basic shortcrust pastry dough and use as a frangipane on little jam tarts.

Golden Milk Custard Tart

Golden blend (page 80)

Serves 8 / Makes 23 cm (9 in) tart

Takes: 1 hr 40 mins, plus overnight chilling
Effort level: A little effort

- 250 g (9 oz/2 cups) plain (all-purpose) flour, plus extra for dusting
- ¼ teaspoon salt
- 20 g (¾ oz/4 teaspoons) caster (superfine) sugar
- 130 g (4½ oz) cold unsalted butter, cubed
- 3 egg yolks
- 1–2 tablespoons cold water

For the filling
- 2½ teaspoons Golden Blend (page 80)
- 450 ml (15¼ fl oz/generous 1¾ cups) double (heavy) cream
- 120 g (4 oz/½ cup) caster (superfine) sugar
- 1 vanilla pod (bean), halved lengthways
- 7 egg yolks
- ¼ nutmeg

Golden milk, also known as haldi doodh in Hindi, or as turmeric milk in popular culture, is a milky drink made with a blend of turmeric, cinnamon and black pepper, and often sweetened with honey. Custard tart is a dessert of simple pleasure – a buttery pastry base, wobbly custard and a nutmeg topping. In this case, the custard takes on the golden milk flavours for a deliciously delicate and unique creamy dessert. Try not to overbake this tart – as tempting as it may be to leave it in the oven longer, the centre should still have a vigorous wobble when tested after the required time.

1. Tip the flour into a food processor, along with the salt, sugar and cubed butter. Pulse to a fine breadcrumb-like texture. Add the egg yolks and 1 tablespoon of the cold water, and pulse until the mixture comes together, adding another tablespoon water if needed. Form into a puck, cover and freeze for 20 minutes.

2. Roll out the pastry on a lightly floured work surface to a thickness of about 3 mm (⅛ in), and use it to line the base of a 23 cm (9 in) fluted tart tin (pan). Freeze for 20 minutes. Meanwhile, preheat the oven to 180°C fan (350°F/gas 6).

3. Fill the tart with a disc of baking parchment and some baking beans, and blind-bake for 15 minutes, then remove the beans and bake for a further 5 minutes. Allow to cool.

4. For the filling, reduce the oven temperature to 130°C fan (260°F/gas 2). Toast the Golden Blend in a dry frying pan (skillet) over a medium heat for 2 minutes, then transfer to a large saucepan and add the cream, half the sugar and the vanilla. Warm through over a medium heat until the sugar has dissolved. Remove and discard the vanilla pod.

5. In a heatproof bowl, using a balloon whisk, whisk together the remaining sugar and the egg yolks, then pour in the hot cream mixture, whisking constantly. Pour this into the baked case and finely grate over the nutmeg. Slide into the lower part of the oven and bake for 30 minutes. The tart should be set with a wobble in the centre; it will set further as it chills.

6. Remove from the oven and leave to cool in the refrigerator for 5 hours, or ideally overnight. It will keep covered in the refrigerator for 4 days.

Extra ideas

- **Easy Golden Blend shortbread biscuits** – In a large bowl, combine 150 g (5 oz/1¼ cups) plain (all-purpose) flour, 100 g (3½ oz) cubed cold salted butter, 50 g (2 oz/¼ cup) caster (superfine) sugar and 2 teaspoons Golden Blend. Using your fingertips, rub everything together until it resembles breadcrumbs, then use your hands to squeeze the dough into a ball. Roll out the dough on a lightly floured work surface until it is 1 cm (½ in) thick, then cut into about 20 equal-sized fingers. Chill for 30 minutes. Preheat the oven to 150°C fan (260°F/gas 2) and line a large baking sheet with baking parchment. Arrange the cookies on the sheet and bake for 15–20 minutes until golden. Leave to cool completely, then store in an airtight container for up to a week.
- Make a basic custard recipe and add 1–2 teaspoons Golden Blend, or stir it through shop-brought custard while warming through.
- Add Golden Blend to rice pudding for the final 5 minutes of cooking.

Masala Chai Ice Cream

Ginger (page 48), **Cardamom** (page 28),
Peppercorns (page 58), **Cinnamon** (page 34)

Serves 6–8

Takes: 1 hr 30 mins–2 hrs, plus 12 hrs freezing
Effort level: A weekend challenge

- 400 ml (13 fl oz/generous 1½ cups) full-fat (whole) milk
- 300 ml (10 fl oz/1¼ cups) double (heavy) cream
- 4 tablespoons loose Assam tea leaves
- 5 cm (2 in) piece of fresh ginger root, peeled and thinly sliced
- 15 cardamom pods, bashed
- 2 cinnamon sticks
- 1 teaspoon ground cinnamon
- 12 cloves
- 3 teaspoons black peppercorns
- 1 vanilla pod (bean), split lengthways
- 6 egg yolks
- 220 g (7½ oz/generous 1 cup) soft light brown sugar

The Indian tea masala chai consists of several basic components – Assam tea, spices and fresh ginger. In India, it is an around-the-clock-beverage that comes black or milky and often sweetened. There is something magical about masala chai: the spices and the rich hit of the black tea are near perfection in their balance. Here, these elements are churned into a silky-smooth ice cream.

1. Pour the milk and cream into a large saucepan. Add the tea, ginger, cardamom, both types of cinnamon, cloves, peppercorns and vanilla, and simmer gently over a low heat for 10 minutes. Turn off the heat and leave to infuse for 30 minutes.

2. In a large bowl, beat together the egg yolks and sugar with a whisk until slightly thickened. Strain the milk mixture through a sieve (fine mesh strainer) into a jug to remove the spices, then slowly whisk it into the eggs and sugar, pouring it into the bowl in a continuous stream. Once incorporated, pour the mixture back into the saucepan and set it over a low heat. Cook gently, stirring constantly, for around 10 minutes, scraping the bottom of the pan as you go. The mixture will slowly thicken into a custard; when it's ready, it will coat the back of a spoon. Set the bowl of custard over a bowl of iced water and stir constantly until the custard has cooled.

3. Churn the custard in an ice-cream maker, following the manufacturer's instructions. Alternatively, pour the custard into a freezerproof container and freeze for 3 hours, removing the container once every hour and blitzing in a food processor. Then freeze again until firm.

4. When the ice cream is frozen, but not too hard, transfer it into a freezerproof container. Cover with a lid and leave in the freezer overnight before serving. Serve in small bowls or ice-cream cones.

Try this

- **Quick masala chai for 4** – Tip 5 bashed cardamom pods, 2 cinnamon sticks, 3 cloves, 3 black peppercorns, 4 teaspoons loose Assam tea leaves, a 3 cm (1¼ in) piece of fresh ginger, peeled and sliced, and 400 ml (13 fl oz/generous 1½ cups) water into a large saucepan. Bring to the boil, then reduce the heat and simmer gently for 10 minutes. Add 400 ml (13 fl oz/generous 1½ cups) milk of your choice and slowly bring to the simmer. Strain and sweeten with honey.

Fennel Seed and Lemon Buttermilk Pound Cake

Fennel (page 42)

Serves 8

Takes: 1 hr 20 mins
Effort level: A little effort

- 220 g (7½ oz) unsalted butter, softened, plus extra for greasing
- 1 heaped tablespoon fennel seeds
- 200 g (7 oz/scant 1 cup) caster (superfine) sugar
- 3 eggs
- finely grated zest of 2 large lemons and juice of 1
- 200 g (7 oz/1⅔ cups) plain (all-purpose) flour
- 1 teaspoon cream of tartar
- 1 teaspoon baking powder
- ½ teaspoon fine sea salt
- 120 ml (4 fl oz/½ cup) buttermilk
- 200 g (7 oz/1⅔ cups) icing (confectioners') sugar

This is one of those simple recipes turned into something truly special by the addition of spice. The liquorice sweetness of the fennel and the lemon zest make it feel sophisticated, with the buttermilk adding a slight acidity to an otherwise sweet cake. Everyone should have a pound cake recipe in their repertoire; it has something of a soft yet rich and tender, comforting texture. It's easy to make and loved by all who have tried it.

1. Preheat the oven to 160°C fan (320°F/gas 4). Grease a 450 g (1 lb) loaf tin (pan) and line the base and sides with 2 wide strips of baking parchment so that they come just above the lip of the tin (this will help you to lift out the cake later).

2. Lightly crush two-thirds of the fennel seeds in a pestle and mortar and set aside. In a stand mixer fitted with a whisk attachment, or using an electric hand-held whisk in a large bowl, beat together the butter and caster sugar at a medium-high speed for at least 10 minutes, or until extremely fluffy. It should have a pale colour and a mousse-like texture. Beat in the eggs, one at a time, until they are all incorporated, scraping down the sides of the bowl with a spatula as you go.

3. In a separate bowl, combine the crushed fennel seeds, lemon zest, flour, cream of tartar, baking powder and salt. Add this to the butter mixture and beat for 20 seconds, or until just combined. Add the buttermilk and briefly mix again. Spoon the batter into the prepared loaf tin and bake for 55–60 minutes (checking after 55 minutes) until the cake is risen and golden and a skewer inserted into the centre comes out clean. Leave to cool completely in the tin.

4. Sift the icing sugar into a large bowl. Add the lemon juice and stir to create a thick icing (frosting), adding more lemon juice if it seems too thick. Remove the cooled cake from the tin and peel off the baking parchment. Spoon the icing gently on to the cake so that it slowly drips down the edges. Finish with the remaining fennel seeds. Leave to stand for 1 hour before cutting into generous slices and serving.

Try this

- Fennel can be added to all sorts of citrus dishes. Try adding 1 teaspoon to homemade lemonade, lemon cookies, the pastry of a lemon meringue pie or in homemade curd.

No-knead Everything Bagel Focaccia

Fennel (page 42), **Caraway** (page 27)

Serves 6–8

Takes: 2½ hrs, plus overnight chilling
Effort level: A little effort

- 6 tablespoons extra virgin olive oil, plus extra for oiling
- 500 g (1 lb 2 oz/4 cups) strong white bread flour
- 400 ml (13 fl oz/generous 1½ cups) lukewarm water
- 10 g (¼ oz/2½ teaspoons) fine sea salt
- 7 g (¼ oz) sachet fast-action dried yeast (2 teaspoons)

For the everything seasoning

- 1½ teaspoons sea salt flakes
- 2 tablespoons poppy seeds
- 1 tablespoon sesame seeds
- 1 teaspoon garlic granules
- ½ teaspoon fennel seeds
- ½ teaspoon caraway seeds

If you've been to New York, it's not unlikely that you've eaten in one of the many bagel joints dotted over the city. You'll find plain, poppy seed, or onion bagels – and a rather curious, delicious number called an everything bagel. This topping is iconic in NYC, and consists of a combination of poppy and sesame seeds, garlic powder and sea salt. In this case, caraway and fennel seeds have been added into the mix. It's a versatile seasoning that's easy to throw together, and particularly moreish atop this squishy, easy-to-make, no-knead focaccia (where most of the work is done in the overnight rising process). Pile pastrami or smoked salmon into two halves of the focaccia for a speedy lunch.

1. For the everything seasoning, mix together all the ingredients in a small bowl and set aside.

2. For the focaccia, oil a large, deep bowl and set aside. Tip the flour into another large bowl, then add the lukewarm water, sea salt, yeast and 3 tablespoons of the olive oil. Mix together until you have a shaggy but lump-free dough. Transfer to the oiled bowl. Cover with cling film (plastic wrap) or a dish towel and leave in the refrigerator overnight to double in size.

3. Once the dough has doubled in size, gently grab one side of the dough and fold it over to the other side, tucking it under until taut. Make sure you are very gentle so you don't knock out any of the air. Turn the bowl 180 degrees and pull the dough up and fold it over itself. Leave for 20 minutes, then repeat this process three times more at 20-minute intervals.

4. Oil the sides of a 23 × 33 cm (9 × 13 in) rectangular baking tin with 1 tablespoon of the remaining oil, then line the base with baking parchment. Tip the dough into the tin and gently stretch it out into the corners. Cover with cling film (plastic wrap) or a dish towel and leave to rise at room temperature for 1–1½ hours, or until risen and filling the tin. Meanwhile, preheat the oven to 200°C fan (400°F/gas 7).

5. Drizzle the remaining olive oil over the risen dough, then use

your fingers to make lots of dimples in the dough's surface. Sprinkle over the everything seasoning. Bake the focaccia for 25–30 minutes until deep golden brown. Leave to cool completely in the tin before slicing.

Quick tips

- Add caraway seeds to a simple cake batter, or try swapping the fennel for caraway in the Lemon and Fennel Seed Pound Cake on page 210.
- Add caraway seeds to a savoury shortcrust pastry. This works particularly well as a base for a cheese and onion tart.
- Quadruple the everything seasoning and keep it in a jar to use as a savoury seasoning or topping. Sprinkle over popcorn, potato wedges or macaroni cheese.

Gouda and Cumin Butter Biscuits

Cumin (page 40)

Makes 16

Takes: 35 mins, plus 40 mins freezing
Effort level: Easy

- 100 g (3½ oz/generous ¾ cup) plain (all-purpose) flour
- 35 g (1¼ oz/⅓ cup) wholemeal rye flour
- 1½ teaspoons cumin seeds
- 100 g (3½ oz) cold unsalted butter, cubed
- 130 g (4½ oz) mature Gouda or Comté, finely grated
- 1 tablespoon cold full-fat (whole) milk
- ¼ teaspoon sea salt

The mature, traditional Gouda produced in the Netherlands is superior to some of the milder, inauthentic versions we find on our supermarket shelves. It is nutty, yet creamy and salty, up there with some of the best cheeses in the world. In most of the cheese shops in the Netherlands, you'll also find some of the older mature Gouda laced with cumin seeds. Its nuttiness and the hit of aroma from the cumin seeds is utterly delicious. These little biscuits are an ode to that cheese. If you can get a good-quality Gouda, great, but if you can't, a hard cheese like Gruyère or Comté will work well. Pair these biscuits with a cold, pale lager or wrap them up in baking parchment for someone as a generous gift.

1. Blitz the flours, cumin seeds and butter in a food processor until the mixture resembles fine breadcrumbs. Add the cheese, milk and salt, and blitz again until it is lumpy and pliable. Using your hands, bring the dough together into a 4 cm (1½ in) log and wrap in baking parchment. Chill in the freezer for at least 40 minutes, or until solid.

2. Preheat the oven to 160°C fan (320°F/gas 4) and line 2 large baking sheets with baking parchment. Unwrap the dough and cut into 16 × 1 cm (½ in) slices. Arrange on the lined baking sheets, spaced well apart (they will spread in the oven), and bake for 25 minutes, or until golden. Leave to cool. Store in an airtight container for 3 days.

Extra ideas

- **Baked cumin rice** – Fry 1 sliced onion in 50 g (2 oz) unsalted or salted butter in a casserole dish (Dutch oven) over low–medium heat for 15–20 minutes until golden and sticky. Add ½ tablespoon cumin seeds and a pinch of ground turmeric. Stir in 200 g (7 oz/1 cup) rinsed basmati rice, 1 bay leaf and 320 ml (11 fl oz/generous 1¼ cups) water. Bring to a simmer, then cover and bake for at 160°C fan (320°F/gas 4) 15 minutes. Leave to stand for 5 minutes before serving.
- Mix cumin seeds into chopped tomatoes, cucumber, salt and mint for a quick salad, or try our Kachumber Salad on page 104.
- Fry cumin seeds in rapeseed (canola) oil or butter, then drizzle over carrot and coriander soup.
- Slice a nutty cheese like Gruyère, Harvati or Gouda and arrange on a plate. Drizzle with honey and sprinkle with cumin seeds before serving with crackers or crispbreads.

Warm Cheddar and Nigella Seed Buns

Nigella (page 51)

Makes 20

Takes: 55 mins, plus 1 hr 30 mins rising and proving
Effort level: A little effort

- 120 g (4 oz) unsalted butter, melted, plus extra for greasing and to serve
- 50 g (2 oz/⅓ cup) polenta (cornmeal)
- 280 ml (10 fl oz/generous 1 cup) full-fat (whole) milk
- 500 g (1 lb 2 oz/4 cups) strong white bread flour, plus extra for dusting
- 7 g (¼ oz) sachet fast-action dried yeast
- 1 heaped teaspoon caster (superfine) sugar
- 1 teaspoon fine sea salt
- 30 g (1 oz) Parmesan or vegetarian hard cheese, finely grated
- 120 g (4 oz/1⅓ cups) mature Cheddar, finely grated
- 2 tablespoons nigella seeds
- vegetable oil, for oiling
- 1 egg, lightly beaten
- mango chutney, to serve

Nigella seeds work very well alongside tangy, salty Cheddar. These buns are fantastic served with a bowl of soup or torn apart and eaten warm, slathered in butter and a dollop of mango chutney. Try them dunked into the Carrot, Turmeric and Tamarind Soup on page 126.

1. Grease a 20 × 30 cm (8 × 12 in) rectangle dish or tin (pan) with butter and dust liberally with the polenta. Warm the milk in a small saucepan over a low heat. Once steaming, remove from the heat and add the butter. Swirl the pan to melt the butter, then set aside to cool to room temperature.

2. In a large bowl, combine the bread flour, yeast, sugar, salt, Parmesan, half the Cheddar and most of the nigella seeds. Make a well in the centre, add the milk and butter mixture, and mix everything together until you have a shaggy dough. Turn out on to a lightly floured work surface and knead for 10 minutes by hand, or 7 minutes in a stand mixer fitted with a hook attachment. Transfer the dough to a lightly oiled bowl, cover with a dish towel and leave to rise in a warm place for 1 hour until doubled in size.

3. Once risen, tip the dough out of the bowl and knock back the air. Divide the dough into 20 walnut-sized pieces, weighing for accuracy if you like. Pinch the bottom of each piece to form it into a ball, then set the balls, pinch-side down, 1 cm (½ in) apart in rows in the prepared tin. Cover with lightly oiled cling film and leave to prove at room temperature for 30 minutes.

4. Preheat the oven to 160°C fan (320°F/gas 4). Brush the buns with the beaten egg, then top with the remaining nigella seeds and the grated Cheddar. Bake for 25–30 minutes, or until golden and firm. Leave to cool for 15 minutes in the tin, then eat while still warm with butter and mango chutney.

Extra ideas

- Add 1 tablespoon nigella seeds and a pinch of chilli (hot pepper) flakes to a cheese scone recipe, then eat them warm with butter.
- Mix into the batter of onion bhajis or pakoras before deep-frying.
- Bake nigella seeds into bread recipes of any kind – soda bread works particularly well.

About the Authors

Esther Clark
Esther Clark is an established and experienced recipe writer, food stylist and editor, based in London. She trained as a chef in her early twenties at Leiths School of Food and Wine before working as a chef on a farm in rural Tuscany and catering at weddings in northern India.

Esther works as a freelancer; previously, she was Deputy Food Editor at one of the UK's leading food brands, BBC Good Food. In 2020, she won the PPA 30 Under 30 recipe-writing award. Her recipes celebrate seasonal eating, comfort, big flavours and easy home-cooking methods.

Her regular clients include *Guardian Feast*, OCADO, *Sainsbury's Magazine*, *Delicious* magazine, Co-op's *Food* magazine, BBC Good Food, *Waitrose Food* magazine, Marks & Spencer's, and many more.

Rachel Walker
Rachel Walker was working on the food desk at the *Sunday Times* when she founded Rooted Spices in 2018. She'd been watching the pace of change in the coffee and chocolate industries, and figured it was time that spices caught up. She began sourcing ethically produced and single-origin spices, growing an award-winning and market-disrupting business. Before founding Rooted Spices, Rachel spent a decade working as a food writer and editor, working across national publications, as well as travelling much of the spice route. She lives in East London with her husband Tom, children Florence and Angus, and Tonka the dog, and continues to research, write and track down the best-tasting, most directly sourced spices she can.
rootedspices.com

Authors' Acknowledgements

Esther Clark
Thank you to Hardie Grant for believing in all things spice, and to lovely Eve and Kajal, two people with whom I had always wanted to work, and who showed so much enthusiasm for this idea from the get-go. Special thanks to our editor, Chelsea, ever patient and kind. You've been wonderful to work with.

Thank you, Rachel, for running such an inspiring spice company and bringing Rooted Spices into my spice rack – your boundless knowledge never ceases to amaze me. You're a writer who exudes more enthusiasm for spice than anyone I've ever known, and it comes through in your fantastic words.

To my friends Rosie Reynolds (aka my mentor extraordinaire), Katie Marshall and Troy Willis, for constant support and inspiration – you're the best.

To Karo, not just a top-notch housemate, but also a fantastic friend. Thanks for always being so unbelievably supportive and so passionate about my work, and for hours of tasting my food. Your advice and recipe critiques have been beyond helpful.

A cookbook isn't made without a team of hard workers – thank you Clare, Troy, El, Caitlin and Anna for all your expertise on giving these recipes second, third and fourth tests! From re-baking pound cakes to tasting wedges of sticky toffee pudding in scorching summer temperatures. I've appreciated your insights on this time and time again. Thanks to Caitlin and Clare again for all your hard graft on the shoots, and to lovely Jodie too.

The wonderfully striking design of this book was created by the fantastically talented Stuart Hardie. It's fab, Stuart – thank you for all your hours of hard work.

Matt Russell, Rachel Vere and Matt Hague – you guys are the dream shoot team, and I'm a lucky gal to have had you involved (like, big time) and I couldn't be happier or more grateful to you all for working on it. Also, you all make me laugh a lot.

Arthur, cheers for eating all my food. Even though it's probably all got 'too much flavour'. I'm only sorry there aren't any pea recipes...next time, I promise.

Thanks Ruth and Lizzie; life is tough at times, but it's easier when you have the loveliest sisters.

My mum and dad, I couldn't name more supportive and genuinely kind people. Thank you, Mum, for always helping me, from washing up during hours of testing to being the biggest creative inspiration of my life. Thank you, Dad, for always listening and advising me so articulately. I'm looking forward to cooking more recipes together and eating them around our little kitchen table – it's really my happiest place to be.

Rachel Walker
Thanks to the team at Hardie Grant – to Eve Marleau and Kajal Mistry for commissioning this book, and particularly to Chelsea Edwards for helping bring it to life. Thank you to the wider team: Matt Russell, Matthew Hague, Rachel Vere and everybody present on the shoot days not only for bringing your individual expertise, but also for helping jiggle a baby while doing so. Thank you to Stuart Hardie for the beautiful design, and to Esther for championing Rooted Spices and lending such talent and creativity to this celebration of spices.

A personal thanks goes to the mother-daughter team Carol and Steph, who run Rooted Spice's warehouse in Durham, for being an ever-steadying presence and bringing daily joy to my working life. Thank you also to Hugh for being such a good friend, and always giving such incredibly valued and honest advice.

I am indebted to Ben Hitchcock for generously sharing his encyclopaedic knowledge of spices, and to Christian Smith for his ongoing guidance, enormous kindness and passion for good words. Thank you to my book club for being such a singularly positive force and the best cheerleaders anyone could ask for. Also, to Anna, Antonia, Elly, Katie, Rose and Steph – for your wisdom and wit, and being such willing and entertaining sounding-boards.

Thank you to my mother and mother-in-law respectively, for showing relentless enthusiasm towards my early kitchen endeavours, and enduring positivity towards all culinary and entrepreneurial enterprises that have followed. Thank you also to my father and father-in-law, for both reinforcing the importance of looking things up or asking someone if you don't know the answer, and employing logic to piece together the facts.

My final thanks goes to Tom, the best person I know: unwavering in support, large of heart, loud of laugh and gleefully gluttonous – cooking together and eating together is one of life's purest pleasures. Also a tentative thanks to Florence and Angus, who contributed very little to the writing of this book, but who make life richer and more delicious than I ever could have imagined.

Index

I

K

L

M

N

O

P

Stockists

For all things spicy

Rooted Spices, UK
(rootedspices.com)

Burlap & Barrel, America
(burlapandbarrel.com)

La Boîte, America
(laboiteny.com)

Gewürzhaus, Australia
(gewurzhaus.com.au)

Diaspora Co, America
(diasporaco.com)

Épices de cru, Canada
(epicesdecru.com)

Mill & Mortar, Denmark
(millmortar.com)

Épices Roellinger, France
(epices-roellinger.com)

For delicious ingredients

Belazu – Incredible for extra virgin olive oil, preserved lemons, rose harissa, etc.
www.belazu.com

Odysea – Greek online shop for high-quality Greek yoghurt, feta, halloumi, olives, honey, molasses, etc.
www.odysea.com

Bold Bean Co – For fantastic jars of giant beans, such as butter (lima) beans and chickpeas.
boldbeanco.com

Brindisa – A Spanish online shop great for rice, pulses, flours, pasta, tinned anchovies.
brindisa.com

Vinegar Shed – For delicious handmade vinegars, oils, salts and tinned fish.
www.vinegarshed.com

Panzers – A North London Deli with an online shop. Good for anything from smoked salmon and bagels to high-quality pasta and chocolate.
panzers.co.uk

Pipers Farm – Wonderful grass-fed and free-range butcher's that delivers nationwide in the UK.
www.pipersfarm.com

Japan Centre – A go-to for all your Japanese ingredients, it's good for noodles, oils and vinegars, Japanese rice, seasonings and miso.
www.japancentre.com/en